TENACIOUS
My Journey from War in Sudan to New Life in America

by Ater Malath

Prologue

The land of my birth is filled with desperate people, and because of America, I am not one of them.

Twenty years after I left as a refugee, I returned to the world's newest nation—South Sudan.

As I walked the streets of the small town of Rumbek, where I was born, I thought about how much had changed, and sadly, had not.

Soon after I arrived in early 2017, dozens of relatives eager to see the prodigal son greeted me with enormous excitement, warmth, and kindness. They butchered goats for feasts to celebrate my homecoming.

My relatives gently chided me, wondering why I was sweating so much. I told them I had spent the past two decades away from the heat of Sudan, in colder climates in the United States, such as Seattle.

Martha, my youngest sister, said I must immediately shed my Western clothes so I would blend in and not attract undue attention out in the streets. South Sudan is not a very safe place, and hasn't been for a long time.

After decades of warfare, the civilian populace is heavily armed. While I visited Rumbek, a man was dragged from his home and shot in front of his family—killed by other men who had a grievance with him.

Even as hot as South Sudan is, people in town no longer sleep outside as they did in years past—it simply is too dangerous. The rural areas are much worse. I wanted to visit the cattle camp near town where my father had taken me as a child during happier times. My sister warned against it. Afraid of rustlers and roving bandits, nervous guards armed with AK-47 automatic rifles patrol the cattle camps.

Poverty is everywhere, and there is virtually no economic development of any significance.

How did a land of such wonderful people fall into such horror?

Civil wars, killing South Sudanese for over fifty years since 1955, occurred first between peoples of the south, resisting repression and genocide from the north, and then between competing ethnic groups following independence. Now, South Sudan again is facing unimaginable suffering.

Drought and societal disruption—as hundreds of thousands of civilians fled violence—has the country facing a terrible famine. People in South Sudan are subsistence farmers; they depend on the crops they grow for survival.

The United Nations Security Council in March 2017 heard that the world was facing the largest humanitarian crisis since formation of the UN in 1945, with more than twenty million people in South Sudan, Yemen, Somalia, and Nigeria facing famine and starvation.

The UN estimated that as many as one million South Sudanese could die if substantially more aid from the international community did not arrive soon. More than one million children are acutely malnourished, including 270,000 who face imminent risk of death.

The issue of refugees is politically divisive in the United States, but the overwhelming majority of refugees simply yearn for a place where they and their children will not starve or die from violence. I know how they feel.

My name "Ater" in Dinka has several meanings, but my favorite is "perseverance." I am a tenacious person—an attribute that helped me survive war, starvation, and the trials of refugee camps. Throughout all my ordeals in Africa, the possibility of one day immigrating to America for a better life drove me on.

When I was nine years old, Sudanese soldiers wiped out the village where I was living with my parents. I never saw them again. With my uncle, I fled barefoot over hundreds of miles of war-torn countryside. I lived in four different refugee camps and nearly starved to death in Nairobi's Kibera, one of the poorest slums in the world.

Hopeless, a chance at new life and resettlement to the United States beckoned. In 1995, I was part of a first wave of children allowed into the US from Sudan, with a later group gaining attention as the "Lost Boys of Sudan."

I arrived as a teenager, alone, in Fargo, North Dakota.

Life as an uneducated immigrant in America is arduous and frightening, without the cultural support from home. With few options, I worked at horrid meat packing plants and a long series of filthy, backbreaking jobs. Mine is an experience of America shared by many fellow refugees.

The following pages recount the story of my life as a member of the Dinka people in South Sudan, of how sectarian and religious hatred shattered my life and broke apart my family.

My story provides a glimpse of the challenges and opportunities faced by refugees who immigrate to the United States.

This is a story of Africa and America.

More than anything else, I hope this book brings attention to the impending human disaster facing the people of South Sudan, and the plight of refugees everywhere.

When South Sudan gained independence in 2011, there was so much hope. What I saw on my recent visit there filled me with despair.

The land of my birth is filled with desperate people.

Millions of people in the world are exactly as I was twenty years ago—desperate for a compassionate hand to reach out and pull them away from a nightmare. According to the UN High Comissioner for Refugess—the UN's refugee agency—the number of refugees in 2015 was more than sixty million—or nearly one in one hundred people worldwide.

I hope this book opens some eyes—and hearts—about conditions in the world experienced daily by far too many of our fellow human beings. It is too easy to retreat to comfortable homes and lives and forget about the overwhelming suffering in the world. Too easy to forget that millions of people need help simply to survive another day.

How we treat our poorest and most vulnerable may say more about us as a civilization than anything else. It is not too late for humanity to embrace its neediest. At least I hope not...

Chapter 1

Life in Rumbek. The Dinka People

I was born on September 25, 1976, in a small town called Rumbek—then with a population of about 10,000—in the nation of Sudan. Rumbek is the capital of Lake State and is 234 miles, 337 kilometers, northwest of Juba, the capital of what is now the Republic of South Sudan. In the downtown area, there were beautiful mahogany, neem, and mango trees, which the British had planted along the streets.

Mahogany trees along Rumbek-Wau Road

The houses there were built with mud, brick, or stone and thatched rooftops. The government buildings, schools, stores, hospital, and the houses of well-to-do people were of either brick or stone and had zinc or tile rooftops. Because South Sudan is close to the equator, it gets hot—eighty to a hundred degrees Fahrenheit—in the summer, but it is a dry heat and is breezy. In the fall, the temperature ranges from sixty to sixty-five degrees Fahrenheit.

I am the firstborn. My father's name was Malath Kuandak Tiok, and my mother's name was Cholhok Mapour Gum. My parents were born and grew up in the Rumbek area and belonged to the Dinka Agaar. All my relatives from my dad's and mom's sides had lived there for their entire lives.

Rumbek Hospital where my father worked

By the time civil war split our family, my dad was in his forties and Mom was in her early thirties. Dad worked at the only hospital in town as a nurse, but my mom stayed home because she had never been to school. She and I often visited my grandmother, Anyon, who lived in the country and grew crops, and we brought home peanuts, mung beans, peas, beans, and many other food items that we did not have in town. Sometimes, my aunt, Chuot, my dad's older sister, came to town and took me to her house in a village called Majok, an hour's walk from Rumbek. I'd spend several days there. Other times, my cousin, Mayak, and I visited Marial Kuandak, my dad's brother, in the country.

It was fun visiting relatives. There, I was able to enjoy things I could not do in town, such as bird watching and chasing birds and monkeys away from eating crops on the farm. I loved the feeling of being free in nature. Most exciting of all was when Dad took me on trips to the cattle camp on his day off work. We walked several hours through forest and across the plain where numerous deer and antelopes often grazed. Once we arrived at the camp, he showed me the cows and bulls that we owned and explained to me in great detail what the children did there.

Cattle camps typically have about 2,000 head of cattle. Boys herd them and do many other chores on the side, such as milking and picking up cow dung. They also take care of the calves after the cattle have been taken to grazing. The calves are not allowed to graze with their mothers until they are mature enough to keep up with them. The boys are required to tie them under trees and feed them with hay. A small boy as young as eight years old may herd hundreds of heads of cattle. After they have been taken to grazing, the boys who are not herding collect the dung from the campsite and scrape it with wood shaped like a rake and let it dry in the sun. In the evening when the cattle return to the camp, they put the dry dung into conical mounts and then light fire to them to produce smoke at night and keep the mosquitoes at bay.

During the night, the cow dung burns down to ashes. In the morning, these young Dinka boys apply it to their skin to protect them from the mosquitoes and tsetse flies. Young men also use it and rub it onto cows for the same purpose.

A girl is allowed to perform boys' duties, such as herding cattle, if she is the only girl. The moment she turns fourteen years of age, she can no longer carry out those activities, even if she does not have a brother, because she is too old to be going alone after cattle.

Dinka is the umbrella of all the Dinka people. I personally do not think of Dinka as a single tribe but as an amalgamation of many, which speak the same dialect with different accents and have similar traditions, culture, and customs. Therefore, the suitable term to describe Dinka is Dinka people.

The Dinka Agar for instance is comprised of five ethnic groups— Aliamtoc one and two, Kuei, to which I belong, Rup, and Pakam. Each of these groups are broken down further into many more clans. The Dinka are pastoralists and farmers. We grow crops on our farmlands. Cattle are kept in the camps a distance of an hours' walk from the villages. Only goats and sheep stay in the villages. Since our cattle are not in enclosures, they need to be kept separate from the farmlands so they can graze freely on the plain, toc. Some people look after them there while others tend to the crops. People go back and forth from the camps and villages, and supply one another with whatever they are lacking in their diets.

In Dinka culture, boys are named after the bulls and girls after the cows. At puberty, a Dinka man receives a name after his ox. This is a very special one—his personality ox. This age, the Dinka men indeed believe they and their oxen are one. The oxen are the completion of their personalities. They take them around in the camp even when they are courting young girls. A bull with a mixture of white and black patches is our favorite color. However, there are many other recognized colors for bulls and each has a little distinction.

In Dinka culture, as many as five or six men may court a girl. However, the man who marries her is the one with the most cattle. He is able to afford the high bride price required by parents to give away their daughters.

We Dinka believe, that of all the people in Africa, we are indeed the most devoted to our animals, and we see our cattle as the most beautiful in the world. We live off their milk, sleep on their hides, and believe our animals have a spiritual connection to God. We are very possessive about our cattle. We rarely kill a cow, a goat, or sheep for consumption, except during special occasions, such as weddings or other festivities. Cattle are for marriage, milk, and butter. The bulls are sold to buy items of importance, such as mosquito nets or grain, or whenever there is a drought and a poor harvest occurs. Occasionally, we sacrifice our animals to get a blessing from God.

During the dry season, we move our cattle quite frequently. We are constantly in search of good pastures, and that explains why we are considered pastoralists and not nomads. When a camp is moved to a different place, the men look after all the young animals and carry small kids on their shoulders. Girls are responsible for carrying on their heads the entire community possessions from camp to camp, sometimes for a distance of many miles. They carefully wrap all the cooking pots and every little small personal item in sleeping hides.

When school started, I took care of the goats and sheep. I woke up very early in the morning and then walked about a mile and half to school barefoot. There were no buses or lunch at school either. As soon as I came home, my mom gave me some food, and would say, "Ater, eat faster so you can take the goats and sheep to grazing. They are hungry."

Whenever she said that, I grew frustrated as I usually was very tired after walking from school and wanted at least an hour to rest before I'd take the goats and sheep to graze along the Rumbek airstrip.

Rumbek airstrip, February 2017

To be honest, those goats and sheep really knew me very well. Whenever they saw me coming home from school, they'd all rise from under the trees where they were tied and cried and peered at me, even when I was eating my food.

Out of curiosity, I asked Mom whether they cried when I was at school. Surprisingly, she told me, "No, they lie down and sleep when you are away. They only cry when they see you coming, because they know they are going to get out soon."

To me, it was as if they were telling me, "Please, don't be so self-centered and eat and neglect us. We want to eat too."

I was a good student and always wanted to do my homework, but I could not tell Mom what I should do. Given that she had never gone to school, goats and sheep had priority over my homework. I herded them from two p.m. to six p.m. When I came home in the evening, exhausted, she would light a kerosene lamp, and say, "Now, make sure you finish your homework." I'd do two or three homework problems, and then often fall fast asleep. Sometimes, we ran out of gas for the lamp and, in that case, I'd not get a chance to do even a single problem. I used to dream of light so I could study more. I was getting poor grades compared to other kids whose parents provided them with an environment more conducive to learning.

Chapter 2

Empty Promises

Sudan is a very diverse country. In the north, there are Arabs who came as settlers, while in the south, east, and west there are many black native tribes. Each of these have its own dialect, tradition, customs, and beliefs.

During the colonial era, the British badly neglected the south. By the time independence came about, creating the nation of Sudan, northerners were far ahead of the south politically, economically, and in education. Like many African nations formed after colonialism, there were built-in tensions.

When the British departed in 1956, they left a democratically elected government for the independent nation of Sudan, but it was a fractured nation, with the seeds of conflict already sown along divisive religious and ethnic lines. The government was mainly for the benefit of the north. Projects promised to help the south catch up with the north's economic development never materialized. The south had only dirt roads. There were few good hospitals or schools. Most of the existing ones had been set up by British missionaries. Due to their advantages, a powerful nationalist movement in the north believed Sudan should remain as a united country despite its cultural, ethnic, and religious diversity.

There was no way the north would grant South Sudan its wish for independence since the country's economic viability was dependent on southern Sudan's abundant resources.

This inevitable conflict, a legacy of British colonialism, and religious and cultural differences, spawned a series of armed conflicts. With northerners dominating everything in the south, anger erupted across the south like wildfire. Southerners did not consider Sudan's "independence" legitimate since the north had benefitted and the concerns of the south were not addressed.

Lack of development and representation in the government led to the first ripples of civil war on August 18, 1955, a few months before independence. Members of the Equatoria Corps, the British-administered defense force, mutinied in the town of Torit in Eastern Equatoria. This mutiny was an expression of angry unrest, and not a well-coordinated uprising.[1]

The first few years of rebellion against the government in the north were limited by a lack of weapons and little backing from other nations, or even much support from the general population, which was a lingering effect of colonization and tribal differences. During the time of the British, some tribes were marginalized and looked down upon, especially pastoralist ones like the Dinka—my tribe—and Nuer.

The British arrogantly thought we were backward and primitive since we moved from place to place seasonally, looking for good pastures for our cattle. In contrast, the sedentary agricultural tribes in Equatoria and Western Bahr el Ghazal, who were farmers, were easily pacified by the British because of their immobility and inability to avoid British military patrols. These tribes were the first to be recruited into security forces by the British. Later on, the British used the Equatorial Corps to carry out the final pacification of the Nuer and Dinka of Bahr el Ghazal and the Upper Nile.[2]

---

1   Douglas Johnson, *The Root Causes of Sudan's Civil Wars* (Bloomington: Indiana University Press, 2003), 28.

2   Johnson, *The Root Causes of Sudan's Civil Wars*, 18.

When regional conflict began with the creation of Sudan as a nation, the pastoralist tribes at first didn't support the Equatoria tribes who fought against the northern government. They believed those tribes had been puppets of the British and did not trust them. For a few years, the rebel force, Anyanya, named after a deadly poison, randomly fought with the few weapons they had captured from the Sudanese Army with help from southerners rebelling and defecting, who joined the rebels.[3] As time progressed, other tribes realized it was not just about Equatoria. All southern tribes were threatened with repressive domination from the north.

On November 17, 1958 a retired military leader, General Abbud, organized a coup against the government, which was led by civilians. Abbud wanted to Islamize the south and crack down on Anyanya. He imposed Islam and Arabic by force and declared Friday as the weekly day of religious observance and rest. He shut down Christian mission schools and transferred them to government control. Christian missionary activities were strictly restricted during Abbud's regime until all were eventually expelled from the country in 1964.[4] The situation in the south became terrible, especially in 1962, as the government burned down villages while attempting to annihilate the Anyanya. More and more people rebelled and joined the Anyanya, and that was the real beginning of the first civil war.

In 1966, General Abbud was overthrown because of his ineffective economic policies—he was more of a military leader. There was a big demonstration in the north, especially in the capital city of Khartoum. Unrest spread all over the country and eventually forced Abbud to step down from power to be replaced by a caretaker government—the civilian

---

3   Johnson, *The Root Causes of Sudan's Civil Wars*, 31.
4   Girma Kebbede. "Sudan: The North-South Conflict in Historical Perspective." Contributions in Black Studies Vol.15, article 3. (1997): 18.

government of Prime Minister Sadig el Mahdi. Regardless of military or civilian government, all successive regimes pursued the common goal of Arabization and Islamization of the entire country. The continued worsening economic and political situation in the country later led to the demise of Mahdi's government in 1969.

In that year, Jaafar Nimeiri led another coup and became the president, but in 1971, members of his own party, the Communist Party, worked in conjunction with discontented army officers and attempted to overthrow him in an abortive coup. After this, Nimeiri went on a rampage. He purged and executed many of his opponents.

Nimeiri was brought into power with the assistance of some southern politicians who hoped he was going to help the south and bring about peace. When he came to power, Nimeiri made a calculated decision to negotiate with rebels, in part because Anyanya had evolved into a lethal force due to external support it received from countries such as Uganda and Israel. Israel provided arms to Colonel Joseph Lagu,[5] the commander who had started the rebellion in Torit.

The Anyanya had factions along tribal lines, but once the main faction, led by Lagu, acquired more weapons and support, the other factions joined, and Lagu was able to influence them. That was when they formed the Southern Sudan Liberation Front, and eventually changed "Front" to "Movement." Southern Sudan Liberation Movement.

Nimeiri proposed a peace agreement with the rebels. He said the people in South Sudan had a right to political, economic, and religious freedom, like other people in the country. Once Lagu heard that, he decided to negotiate. Leaders of many African nations, especially neighboring countries that were experiencing a tremendous influx of

---

5   Johnson, *The Root Causes of Sudan's Civil Wars*, 36-37.

refugees due to the civil war, strongly encouraged Nimeiri and Lagu to bring the war to an end. The result was the Addis Ababa Agreement, which took place in 1972.

The Addis Ababa Agreement granted southern autonomy. It provided a regional government, which meant the south was to have a legislative and executive council that would take care of affairs there. The Addis Ababa Agreement gave the southern regional government powers to raise revenues from local taxation and guaranteed additional money from the central government.

The southern regional government created by the Addis Ababa Agreement could vote to request the president of the republic exempt the southern government from any national legislation it considered unfavorable to the southern regional interest.[6] The agreement gave the south everything, except control over economic planning and anything to do with national defense.

When the opposing parties came to the negotiating table in Addis Ababa, each side had to compromise, but there continued to be deep distrust. The Anyanya wanted the rebel army to stay separate in the south. The south proposed two armies—one for the south and another for the north. The north rejected that proposal. Therefore, they decided an equal number of southern rebels and northern soldiers would be stationed in the south and not transferred north. That process of absorbing the ex-Anyanya would take five years.[7]

From 1972 to 1982, there was a relative peace and the conflict calmed down. In the Addis Ababa Agreement, the government promised to develop the south to bring it to the level of the north, but nothing was implemented. It was only in theory. It was nothing but a lie.

---

6   Johnson, *The Root Causes of Sudan's Civil Wars*, 40.
7   Johnson, *The Root Causes of Sudan's Civil Wars*, 40.

In the south, we became increasingly dissatisfied as we found ourselves in a far worse situation socially and economically than we had been before the Addis Ababa Agreement. We naively had expected the government to implement everything it had committed itself to in the agreement, but it deliberately chose not to carry out any meaningful reforms or economic development in the south. The infrastructure remained as poor as it was before the peace agreement was signed.

Chapter 3

The South Fights Back

The roads all over the south were and are made of dirt; driving on them is extremely difficult during the rainy season. Although the number of primary schools increased somewhat during Nimeiri's regime, most lacked even basic facilities. They did not have bus or transportation systems. Children walked. I remember, after we moved out of Rumbek to Mabuoi in 1984 because of war, I walked about six miles to and from school every day.

Ager Gum primary school (formerly Madina)

Many schools did not have adequate classrooms, so school officials made students in grades one to three attend classes under trees. We had few textbooks, and as many as five students shared one book. They brought their own snacks from home. Those whose parents were poor and could not afford to provide them with some pocket money went hungry all day. I remember running from the school to the hospital where my dad used to work, which was over a mile away, just to get coins to buy roasted peanuts during lunch break. I often sat in class, thinking about food and did not focus on what the teacher said.

The hospital used generators because there was no electricity. The lights would sometimes go out, and the nurses used lamps and flashlights as alternatives. There was no public transportation, no buses whatsoever. People were transported by trucks as commodities. They paid fares and sat on top of them, and when they went sixty mph, the dust would engulf passengers, and you could only see someone's eyes and nose; the rest was covered in dirt.

The central government did plan some projects for the south, but failed to implement most of them. Some were the Nzara and Mongalla textile projects, the Malakal paper industry, the Wau brewery, the Tonj Kenaf, Melut, and Mongalla sugar projects, the Kapoeta cement factory, and the Beden electric plant.[8] A major factor that significantly undermined the Addis Ababa Agreement, and contributed to the breakout of the second civil war, was construction of the Jonglei Canal.

In the mid-1970s, Sudan and Egypt came up with a plan to construct the Jonglei Canal, which would drain the Sudd swamps into the Nile River to increase the discharge of Nile water for agricultural usage in northern Sudan and Egypt. The pastoralist tribes of Dinka, Nuer, and Shilluk had

---

8   John Garang, The Call for Democracy in Sudan (New York: Kegan Paul International, 1992), 31.

for centuries been relying on the Sudd for grazing and water for their herds during the dry season. In 1977, construction of the canal began despite vehement opposition from the southern regional government and local populace, who regarded this project as a destruction of their environment and a threat to their livelihoods. Fortunately, the canal was started but was never completed. The Sudan People's Liberation Army, the SPLA, within a few months of the resumption of the civil war forced a stop to the massive excavation project.[9]

In 1979, Chevron discovered an estimated five billion barrels of oil reserves in Bentiu in the Upper Nile province and Southern Kordofan regions. As soon as oil was discovered, Nimeiri attempted to deprive the south of that precious resource. He tried to redraw the boundaries between the south and north to ensure the areas with oil fell within the northern territories.[10]

That was a clear violation of the Addis Ababa Agreement, which mandated that the boundaries of southern Sudan were to remain as they were drawn from the date of independence from the British. After failing in his effort to annex oil-rich areas, Nimeiri devised another tactic—to build a pipeline from the south all the way to Port Sudan on the Red Sea in the north, despite loud southern regional government opposition.[11] The southern government argued that the government should build refineries in Bentiu, where oil was found, to create jobs and development for the local population.

Sporadic rebellions in the army continued. Ex-Anyanya soldiers and officers weren't given good positions in the reconstituted one. In May 1983, Southern Battalion 105, stationed in Bor Town, led by Commander

---

9   Kebbede, "Sudan: The North-South Conflict in Historical Perspective," 22-23.
10   Kebbede, "Sudan: The North-South Conflict in Historical Perspective," 21.
11   Kebbede, "Sudan: The North-South Conflict in Historical Perspective," 22.

Kerubino Kuanyin Bol, was attacked after they refused to be transferred to the north because that wasn't specified in the Addis Ababa agreement. The northern government was afraid of the southern army being in the south. When the southern battalion refused, the government sent the northern army to disarm them, but they resisted and battle broke out, sparking the second civil war. There were several coordinated mutinies in Ayod, Pochalla, and Pibor, led by Commander William Nyuon Bany Machar.

Army officer John Garang was sent from Khartoum to calm down the mutineers, but that was what he wanted. After he arrived, he joined them, and they marched to Ethiopia to form the Sudan People's Liberation Army. All the battalions that went into the bush rallied around Colonel John Garang De Mabior as their leader.

After the rebellion, the northern government went berserk. They abolished the Addis Ababa Agreement. They divided the south into three separate regions. They dissolved the southern regional government. Nimeiri took a radical step and sided with the Muslim Brotherhood, and transformed the country into an Islamic state. Everywhere in the south there was political unrest and suppression of the local population.

On July 1983, the soldiers who had gone to Ethiopia and formed the SPLA, led by John Garang, fought back. In September 1983, Nimeiri issued a set of decrees, the September Laws, imposing Sharia Law on everybody, Muslim and non-Muslim alike, and that was his final death blow to the Addis Ababa Agreement. He imposed that law without consulting his own party, Sudan Socialist Unions, or People's Assembly. The Addis Ababa Agreement stipulated that Muslims, Christians, and indigenous peoples had equal rights and freedom to worship whatever religion they wished.

Depending on the crime, violators of Sharia Law are punished by hanging, flogging, stoning of women for adultery, or amputation of limbs for crimes such as theft. Most victims of this law were non-Arabs, non-Muslim poor from the south—Darfur and the Nuba Mountains. That strict interpretation of Islam was criticized by many Muslim scholars in the north, calling it "localized" or "political" Islam. In other words, the form of Sharia Law that Nimeiri imposed on the Sudanese people did not fit the recognized interpretation.

Although a few months of civil war were marked by infighting, the decision Nimeiri took to introduce his version of Sharia Law united all the warring southern factions and forced many people to join the SPLA and wage war against the northern government.

The expanding conflict would soon tear apart my family and lead me down many unforeseen roads.

Chapter 4

Violence Close to Home

Civil unrest kept getting worse and worse. Students staged demonstrations and protests in Rumbek and across the south. They used stones and clubs to attack government buildings.

When I was in primary school in 1983, there was a violent fight I witnessed in downtown Rumbek, in the market, between secondary school students and Arab merchants. I had gone into a shop at about ten a.m. to buy a pastry, similar to a croissant. I watched as secondary school students attacked a store, throwing stones and sticks. They hated the Arab merchants.

One of the students, Chol Amerdit, picked up a big, heavy piece of equipment the merchants used to weigh items. I knew Chol. He was a giant, the size of a football player in America. He flung the equipment at one of the Arab merchants, hitting him in the forehead, splitting his face and skull. Blood and brains were everywhere; it was frightening and awful. The Arab quickly died. Another store owner pulled out a long knife—the Arab merchants kept them hidden in their robes—and stabbed Amerdit through the chest, instantly killing him. The police came after that.

I was a little boy, only seven years old. I was terrified and did not know why that was happening. *Why, why, why are these people fighting?* I thought.

That same year the president of Sudan, Jaafar Muhammad Niemieri, visited Rumbek, and everyone went to the airstrip to welcome him. We waited for hours until military helicopters landed on the grass.

Our local people warmly greeted the president. Elders sacrificed cows for his visit. The sacrifice of a bull is a tradition in animist culture. They sacrifice a white one, which is a sign of purity and peace. These sacrifices meant different things for different occasions. In this instance, it was for his respect and protection from harm. As was the tradition, the president stepped over the sacrificed bulls. He went to his car and then drove slowly toward town, waving.

Later, I heard there had been a secret plot to assassinate the president during his visit. While nothing came of it, his speech to people at the town stadium was interrupted by high school students. Just as he began to speak, they chanted, mocking the president because he had done poorly in school. That infuriated the president and he immediately left town and flew back to Khartoum. Later, the radio announced that the government was shutting down Rumbek's secondary school. Many of the high school students left to join the rebellion. That was the start of more civil unrest. People talked about overthrowing the government.

Mom and I worked on the farm during the weekdays after I came back from school. Since Dad worked at the hospital from Monday through Friday, he was only able to work on the farm during the weekday evenings and full time on the weekends, when he was off.

The harvest time was one of the busiest seasons of the year. The first consisted of quick-yield crops such as peanuts and sorghum-types of grain. Those crops took only three to four months, from May to September.

I helped my parents uproot the peanuts. We cured them for several days before separating the nuts from the stalk before we put them into big containers and later sacked them. Every now and then, I'd stop work for a while and take fresh peanut leaves to the goats and sheep to eat where they were tied under the trees. When the sun became hot, we worked in the shade.

In May 1984, about 470 local junior and high school students quit school and joined the rebellion. Six days later, a larger number, 2,060 of them, including teachers and government officials, joined the rebel SPLA. A few teachers who I knew were Majok Mangar Machiek, a university student and a primary school teacher, Bilal Mayaia, Philip Kot, administrator in the town of Yarol, Amuri Dhel, and Marco Chol Machiec, principal at Wau technical school.

The northern government military cracked down on people in town. They hired spies from within the communities and among the students to track those who secretly organized students to quit school and join the rebels. I was too young back then to fully understand what was going on in my hometown, but I vividly remember the obvious incidents like protests and clashes between students and Arab merchants. The security force's crackdowns were hard for me to comprehend. It was just frightening.

I did notice ominous changes in the community, though. People stopped walking around at night, afraid of being stopped by northern security personnel. If the security force discovered a person walking at night—even if he was just going to innocently hang out with friends— they forced that person into their armored personnel carrier, took him to the army barracks of Malou, and tortured him. People kept disappearing for no reason.

At that time, my dad worked as a nurse at the hospital in Rumbek. The town had only one with one physician. Dad traveled around the area on his bicycle to help treat people with diseases and to vaccinate kids for polio. He was very well-respected in my hometown. He treated everybody in need.

Before the conflict, my dad worked the nightshift, and whenever he was done, at around three a.m., he'd ride his bicycle home. As the situation worsened, he stopped coming to the house early when it was still dark. He waited until seven a.m. and then came home.

Nobody took the time to explain to me or the other kids what was actually going on. The adults simply thought we were children so it was unnecessary for us to understand the situation.

The government terrorized our community. In one particularly horrible and cruel incident, the government security force accused a disabled resident named Choruel Pieth Mungu of helping the rebels, saying he was responsible for organizing students to join the rebels. Since he was in a wheelchair and could not take up arms, the security force said he was acting as liaison between the SPLA and those who wanted to join the rebellion.

They took him to the barracks in Malou, which is about seven miles from Rumbek, and tortured him. After, they tied him onto pegs so he could not move and finally set a huge fire all around him until he burned to death. They killed him in that manner to intimidate people from joining the rebels. However, it had the opposite effect; more and more people kept leaving town and joining SPLA.

After the government realized their methods of crude intimidation were not effective, they switched to different tactics. Whenever they received information that people had left town to join the rebels, the army sent soldiers out to lay in wait and ambush them. According to my cousin, when he and other students left town on their way to the Ethiopian border, in a village called Ajwara between Pibor and Pochalla, they fell into a government ambush, and 180 of them were killed and many wounded.

By 1984, many civilians and students had rebelled and joined the SPLA. The rebels raided into Rumbek, so my family moved to a village called Mabuoi, which is about three miles from downtown Rumbek. The government continued its constant threats and violence against the local populace, who they believed were giving support to the rebels by harboring them and supplying them with food.

While we were still living in Mabuoi, other children and I encountered six rebels in a neighbor's house, drinking grain alcohol. They had AK-47 rifles, brown hats and uniforms, and steel-toed boots. That was the first time I had seen rebels. At first, I was nervous and frightened, but in the end, we mustered up the courage to respond to them after they talked to us in Dinka, our dialect. We relaxed once we realized they were not going to do us any harm. They were so friendly. They asked if we wanted to fight the government, and offered us liquor and food. We told them we were still children, so we could neither fight nor drink hard liquor.

The rebels insisted we should eat with them, so we did. At around five in the evening, they said, "Guys, we're leaving." They walked north. My friends and I went back to our houses, and then mysteriously—I don't know if someone told the government soldiers—an armored personnel carrier drove to the airstrip and fired a shell in the direction of that house, just a few minutes after we had left.

After that incident, my dad said we had to move again. He said it would be a good idea to get away from town. He thought living farther away would be much safer. The SPLA combatants made themselves known throughout Rumbek and the surrounding villages by raiding the army garrison and warning civilians to evacuate the town. Early in 1985, we moved from Mabuoi to Yar, which is approximately nine miles from Rumbek.

That meant the end of my schooling. It was too dangerous for me to travel on the road. By 1985, many students left school. It was too risky for civilians to continue living in town, and a lot of people moved to outlying villages. We took our goats and sheep, moved to Yar, and planted crops.

Without school, my life was filled with work. I kept wondering when the war was going to stop so I could go back to classes. I thought the move to Yar was going to be temporary, that we would be able to return to the town soon so I could resume my schooling. However, my dad said it was not possible. He said, "Ater, the first civil war that lasted for almost seventeen years, from 1955 to1972, started gradually as this one, but it kept getting worse and worse. This current unrest, I believe, will probably last longer than the first civil war."

I said to myself, *My dream is never going to come true.* I wanted to be a doctor, something my father hadn't achieved.

In that village, the rebels sometimes stopped by for food, so my mom prepared some for them. Occasionally, they preferred a goat or sheep instead. Even if Mom offered them something else, they refused, insisting on getting a goat or sheep until Dad slaughtered one, and Mom cooked it for them. One group of rebels came by to ask for a goat, and a few days later, another group came and did the same thing. They nearly finished off all our goats and sheep.

They were disrespectful—they didn't just ask Mom to offer them a goat; they'd pick the ones they liked. Usually, they chose my favorite ones that I did not want to be killed. I wept whenever they grabbed one of those goat or sheep and made Dad kill it.

After we moved to Yar, my dad still rode his bicycle to town, but eventually it became too dangerous. My mom said to Dad, "Forget about your job. We can just grow crops." So he quit. He still occasionally went into town for supplies, though.

I held on to my dream to continue my education. That was what I wanted, but I didn't know the means to do so. I wanted to be a doctor, but didn't know how to become one. The disruption caused by the war was a big, big problem. We lived in Yar until April 1985, when the water pump incident happened. In late April, two days before it, the SPLA had attacked the town of Rumbek.

Chapter 5

The Water Pump Incident

Children in the village of Yar routinely fetched water from the water pump. While parents were busy planting or weeding crops in the field, it was the children's duty to get water from either the wells or water pumps. Our parents would say, "Take the jerry cans and go and get water."

Water pump

One day while I and the other children were in queue, waiting to fill our containers, I heard a loud sound like a jet engine fly low over our heads. A mortar shell landed approximately a hundred meters from the pump. Before that, I had only heard guns from a distance. This one was different. This was not like thunder; it was not a rumbling sound—it was like a tree branch breaking in a rainstorm. We thought lightning had struck, but how could lightning strike without a cloud or rain? We were very confused and terrified by that strange sound, but knew enough to drop to the ground. Some fragments of the shell fell around us. It felt like raindrops. A few seconds after the shell exploded, my dad came running toward me, shouting, "Ater! Come on! Come on!"

The government soldiers thought rebels lurked in the villages surrounding Rumbek, so they drove halfway between Rumbek and Yar. They fired mortar shells randomly in every direction, regardless of civilians. We were shocked. We were trying to make sense of what was going on.

Afterward, we just ran. We came home, packed our belongings, and fled to a cattle camp called Achien, about an hour's walk from Yar. That was what the villagers did in response to the attacks. They ran away, only returning when the government troops had stopped shelling. The following day, we returned to Yar and lived in peace for a couple of months, but it was not to last.

Whenever the SPLA attacked or raided the government army forces in Rumbek, the following day the government soldiers left town and retaliated on local people. They burned down nearby villages, killed innocent civilians, and raped women.

These massacres were not covered by the news media. Government media was just propaganda, and the government didn't allow foreign journalists to come in and report on what was going on in the country.

Even if journalists had been free to cover the atrocities the government committed, it would have been very difficult for them to accurately report on what happened due to security threats and government lies. The government killed our people and blamed it on the rebels or attributed the deaths to tribal violence. It was not until after the signing of the 2005 Comprehensive Peace Agreement between South and North Sudan that foreign journalists were able to really report on Sudan's issues, especially in the south.

In 1985, government soldiers systematically destroyed the villages near Rumbek. The government either massacred or displaced people from Yar, Madhog, Wau Jadit, Adol, Madiing, Majok Aber, Nyangkot, Akol Jal, Makuriric, Akan Aluieny, and Abarkhou.

I will never forget the day the government soldiers attacked Yar. I was nine years old. It was the beginning of the planting season, during May 1985, so my parents were planting crops in the field, along with almost everybody in the village. It was early, around seven in the morning. All of a sudden, I heard loud noises and thought some of our neighbors were beating metal containers or something. I ran outside and saw a house burning and people running across the farm toward ours.

I heard gunshots and mortars, and noticed smoke from surrounding villages. The government soldiers had come out of Rumbek once again and shelled the villages. After the shelling, came troops on foot.

The soldiers did not look like us; they had lighter skin. Almost all of them were Arabs. They wore green uniforms with beret-style hats. They had big rifles with banana ammunition clips. They had left their cars and had quietly walked to our village so we did not hear them coming. That was how they surprised us.

The soldiers were determined to wipe out everything they saw. Homes around my house were in flames. People screamed. They shot people, goats, sheep, chickens, everything in sight. It was complete chaos. I couldn't believe what was going on. I was terrified and disoriented. I thought everybody in the village was going to die that day. I panicked and ran. Everything happened in a flash. There was no time to search for loved ones; you just ran to save your own life.

Once I had reached the tall grass, I dived in and looked back at my home. The government troops walked in the farmlands and village, shooting at everything and anything that moved. People just fled, and the village was deserted. Many ran to the tall grass near the village as well; six hid with me, including my uncle, Mangar, the cousin of my mom.

We lost everything that sustained us. They killed all our goats, sheep, and chickens. They burned the houses with all the grain in them. It was like the end of our world, because even those who survived the massacre now had nothing to live on. People in South Sudan are subsistence farmers; we depend on the crops we grow for survival. When that atrocity happened, we became homeless. I was afraid, sad, and outraged at what they had done to us.

After we fled Yar, we kept running. We knew our territory; we knew every tree in the forest. The government soldiers did not know the surrounding area. They relied on others, collaborators, whom they paid for information on locations. Most people took off to Ethiopia. We had no reason to stay; since our crops had been burned and our animals killed, we had no food.

We crossed the marshland between the villages and the cattle camps. It took us about an hour and a half to get to a cattle camp called Jeu, where we met a group of displaced people from Northern Bahr el Ghazal. My uncle found out that that group was headed to a refugee camp in Ethiopia, and we decided to join them.

I did not know any of those people. They were from a different town, Aweil, which is located in northwestern South Sudan, near the international border with North Sudan and the Abyei Region. They were from the Dinka people like us, but from different clans. They were displaced by the Murahaleen. The government in Khartoum back then armed and trained ethnically based militias and granted them impunity to murder, rape, forcibly displace, and loot property from civilians. Those government-armed Arab militias were called the Murahaleen, meaning "travelers" in Arabic.

The government accused the people of Aweil of supporting the rebellion, just as they had us in Yar and people across the south. The Murahaleen attacked the SPLA and the Dinka people, who were seen as rebels. The Murahaleen came on horseback, and massacred villages. The government of Sudan allowed the militias to take slaves. When the SPLA became stronger and was able to fight back more effectively, the Murahaleen stopped their assaults on Dinka villages and turned to attacking the people of Darfur, and changed their name to the Janjaweed militias.

The people we met in the cattle camp had been displaced like us; they rested in there in Dinka Agaar territory on their way to Ethiopia. Their arrival coincided with the destruction of our village. Despite the fact we did not know one another, we shared two things—we were all refugees and our goal was to get to safety in Ethiopia. When Mangar found out that group headed to Ethiopia as well, he decided we should join them. A journey there was much safer when it was done with a larger group of people.

We left Jeu and went toward a small town called Akot. The group kept getting bigger and bigger as people who had survived the massacres heard about this big group heading to Ethiopia and kept joining us. We walked in single file, alternating adults and children so we did not lose anyone. In the evening, around five o'clock, after we had been walking all day without eating anything and drinking water from ponds, the entire group stopped for a head count. The group was about 350, but eventually it reached almost 400. About a third of us were children.

After we arrived in Akot, Mangar told me that we were going to Ethiopia to live in a refugee camp where the United Nations Refugee Agency, the UNHCR, could provide us with food. He assured me the camp would be much safer than going back to our village. Akot was the starting point of our two-month walk to Ethiopia.

We didn't stay in Akot long because it was on the road. The government jets flew by, searching for people walking on the roads. They bombed refugees or directed military in pursuit. The day we left Akot was a very emotional one. Akot was where my tribe, the Dinka Agaar, still bordered with other Dinka. That was it. We were leaving that behind and were just moving to Ethiopia.

The day we left, I told myself, *Stick with your uncle, and at the same time, take these adults as your parents and listen to what they tell you as you would listen to your mom and dad, or else you won't make it.* That was what motivated me to keep going.

I knew from my uncle that our destination was the Itang refugee camp, but I didn't know how far it was or that it was going to take two months to walk there until later on. In Dinka culture, adults don't explain everything to children. In this case, adults did not tell children how long the journey would take. They thought we might lose hope and not want to walk that far. Even when we were faced with a seven-hour walk, the adults told us it was only three hours, so we'd walk more quickly and not give up. I did overhear adults talking about Ethiopia; they said it was going to be a long and arduous journey.

From that point on, I never saw my parents again. I was nine years old.

Chapter 6

Journey to Ethiopia

Throughout our journey to Ethiopia, so many things affected us, such as a poor diet, bad weather conditions, and diseases. Our diet consisted mainly of meat. That was the only thing people we met could provide us. It was planting season so the grains of last season were in short supply. Whenever we arrived in a village, villagers offered us goats or sheep. We cooked it by itself, without salt or anything else, just meat and water. I was not used to eating only that. Often when I woke up from sleep, I shook, a result of lack of carbohydrates.

I badly missed my parents and everything they used to provide for me. All the food my mom had given me crept into my mind whenever I ate that monotonous meat. Every morning my mother had prepared me a milk tea along with either makuanga, peanut butter, or just salted roasted peanuts. At noon, she came home and prepared a lunch, which usually consisted of assida, a starch made from flour, kissra, a pancake-like type of bread, meat, and mulokhia/khdura, a type of vegetable, or okra.

I constantly wondered about what had happened to my parents. I feared they were dead. Thinking about them made me worry, and I lost my appetite and did not eat. My uncle said, "Ater, don't worry. They're probably okay. They ran just like we did."

My parents had run north while Mangar and I had ran south. Had we gone in the same direction, we might have crossed paths with them several days later. My uncle did not want to go back and look for them. He was determined to take me to the refugee camp.

I now believe my uncle wanted me to go to Ethiopia so I could be safe there and get an education. I don't regret his decision. That was why I got one, because of my uncle. At the time, I was sad but kept moving forward.

The weather was horrible. South Sudan experiences heavy rain in May, June, July, and August. A downpour for just half an hour left floodwater sitting for days. We walked at night to avoid government aircraft spotting us. During the day, we stayed in secluded areas, under big trees and away from roads. We slaughtered goats or sheep offered to us by local people, cooked the meat, ate, and rested. Once the sun set, we resumed walking like the hyenas at night. We walked through the rain and darkness.

Some nights, when there was moonlight and it was clear with no rain, I could see well in front of me as I walked. When dark clouds moved in with rain or drizzle, it grew so dark I could not see the person in front of me. Only when there was lightning, could I see four, five people ahead of me. All we did was feel the path with our feet, and stick to the footsteps of the person in front of us.

A benefit to walking at night was that mosquitos did not bother us as much as during the day. During the walk to Ethiopia, mosquitos often fed on us. Usually, we walked six to seven hours a night unless we did not find a dry place to sleep. If we did not, we continued moving on, even though everybody was tired and ready to stop. I remembered occasions when we spent a long time searching in the darkness, without flashlights, for higher ground and did not find anything.

We did not have shoes either, which made walking much harder. Thorns pricked my bare feet, causing sudden, excruciating pain, but I simply sucked it up and moved on or else I would be left behind. Whenever we took off every evening, I looked at the sky to check if there were clouds that could produce rain. When I saw a dark cloud, I prayed for it not to rain. I hated it when it rained. It complicated everything. In that region of South Sudan, it's mainly plains, no mountains, and when it rains, it pours, and the water pools. In June, there was heavy rain, water, and floods.

At night when we walked, we often heard frogs. As we passed them, they'd quiet, and once we left them behind, they erupted loudly again. We walked through changing terrain. Some places we traveled through a dense forest full of all kinds of creatures. Other times, we crossed flood plains where herds of animals roamed in multitude.

As we headed toward the Nile River, after we left the village of Adior near the town of Yarol, we ventured into a very dense jungle. We stayed on the path through it all the way to the Nile. Local people used that path to get to the Nile for fishing or hunting wild game. While we walked, we heard strange sounds deep in the bush. Birds and insects produced weird noises I had never heard before. Some birds' singing was so pleasant I briefly stopped to listen. Others were so eerie and weird I just wanted to get away from them as fast as possible.

We also heard wild animals, such as hyenas, owls, and elephants. Once I stepped onto fresh elephant's dung. I did not hear lions roaring. I guess that was because dense forest like that is not a lion's habitat. They prefer to live in the savannah where they can chase their prey.

The jungle gradually decreased as we approached the Nile. Soon after we came out of the jungle, we found ourselves on a vast flood plain. Thomson's Gazelles, Tiang Antelopes, and many other game animals roamed there in large numbers.

My uncle decided we should make a camp and take advantage of the abundance of game. The rebels had given him an AK-47 rifle so he could provide protection for the refugees along the way to Ethiopia. He shot antelope. At first, people fought over the meat, but he kept shooting one antelope after another. Every time he killed one, people ran to it with their knives and then chopped up the meat within minutes. I wanted to run in there too and get some for us, but he said, "Stay here with me. We will get our meat later."

I like liver and kidneys. Every time he shot an animal, I asked my uncle, "Can you ask them to leave us a liver and kidneys please?" Later on, when people came back with meat, they gave liver, kidneys, and some meat to my uncle. I cooked for both of us.

Once we had more than enough meat, we decided to cure the rest for future consumption. We cut it thin and long and placed it on little shrubs to dry in the sun. After it was completely dried, we packed it into plastic bags so it would not be spoiled by water. We spent almost a week there.

While we were at that camp, the mosquitos swarmed us and made life miserable. They were relentless, always present. I'd wipe my face and smear bugs all over it. We slept on blankets and sheets. During the night, we built fires and put green leaves on them to produce heavy smoke to keep the insects away. It scared them for a while, but as soon as the fire died down, the mosquitos resumed their vicious assault and we would put more leaves onto the flames. Overnight we had great trouble sleeping because of mosquitos.

Throughout our journey, many people contracted various diseases; numerous children contracted malaria because of mosquito bites. I caught a dose of it, but quickly recovered from it.

We drank from stagnant water that we shared with wild animals, which exposed us to a parasitic worm disease. I got this worm, and so did other refugees. It came to the point where I'd eat and then throw up a few hours later.

I did not get treatment for this worm disease until we reached the Itang refugee camp in Ethiopia. After we arrived, I went to the clinic where an Ethiopian doctor who worked for the UNHCR decided to do a test. He gave me a tiny plastic bottle and asked me to go to the bathroom and get him a tiny sample of stool. After finishing the test, he told me that I had a parasitic worm in my stomach. He prescribed me some medicine and said to me, "Eat some meat, not a lot but just a little bit, and then take the medicine right away."

I did what the physician instructed me to do, and the following morning, I defecated a bunch of worms that looked like spaghetti. After that, my health returned.

There was a tiny flea called thor, similar to fruit flies, which also bothered us along with the mosquitos. Whenever we passed by a herd of animals these fleas were around and jumped into our hair or tried to get into our ears. You'd never outrun them. They were very annoying.

Other people contracted guinea worm disease from drinking contaminated water. The guinea worm got into people's guts as a tiny parasite. As time progressed, it grew about a meter long. This growth process took approximately six months to a year. Once matured, it emerged in a person's lower body, usually in the feet, legs, knees, or groin. The victim experienced excruciating pain, swelling, and then a blister formed, and finally the worm emerged, looking like a white piece of noodle.

About a year after we arrived in the Itang refugee camp, cases of guinea worm disease showed up. Those who had worms in their legs or feet spent a considerable amount of time by the riverside, soaking their feet in the water. They tied a piece of thread onto the worm and then tied it around their legs to prevent it from pulling itself back into the body. They sat in the water and slowly pulled on the worm by wiggling the thread, making sure it did not break. When that happened, the worm disappeared from that blister and later emerged from a different part of them. Once it became too hard to pull, they stopped, tied back the thread around their legs, and went home for the day. That painstaking process continued for days until the worm was completely out of the body.

Chapter 7

Crossing the Nile

After our meat dried completely, we left the camp and headed to the Nile. Once we arrived there, we found no fishermen to ferry us across the river. They had disappeared. They had become fed up with ferrying hundreds of refugees across the Nile; they saw that work as a distraction from their daily occupation of fishing since refugees did not pay them. They had heard about our arrival and hid to avoid taking us to the other side of the river.

We spent several days stuck at the Nile. Fortunately, one day about noon we spotted a fisherman, rowing his canoe along the river. Everybody started shouting, "There is one boat over there."

Mangar shot several rounds from his rifle into the air and said to the man, "Come over here right now." The fisherman was scared to death; he thought we were going to kill him. Our presence surprised him—if he had known about us being at the shore, he probably would have stayed away, just as his fellow fishermen had.

Mangar threatened him and demanded he show us where the other fishermen were. At first, he pretended as if he did not know their whereabouts, but Mangar continued his threats. He told him, "If you do not show us where your people are hiding, I will kill you. It is up to you if you want to die or show us where they are and live."

The fisherman said to Mangar, "I will show you where they are." Everybody was excited. We finally could cross the river if more fishermen showed up with more canoes. Mangar got into the canoe with him, and they rowed away. Half an hour later, they returned with ten fishermen along with their long boats.

The fishermen lived along the Nile and on little islands in the middle of the river. They fished and grew maize, corn. They hunted wild game as well, and were excellent swimmers—able to hold their breath for a long time under water. They opened their eyes when they dove to see what creatures were in their surroundings.

Since there were so many people in the group, about 400 now, the fishermen had to help us cross in their boats first to an island in the middle of the river.

As I crossed the Nile in a canoe, I saw a hippo nearby as it came to the surface and blew water out of its nose. I was fascinated, but as soon as it went under water, many in the boat loudly worried it would try to knock us over.

While the fisherman directing our boat reassured us that we were safe, other stories I later heard from them made me very afraid of hippos. According to them, a hippo does not bite underwater. They said it usually bites its victim on the surface. When a person is swimming, a hippo pushes its victim up into the air with its big nose, waits for a person to land in its massive jaws, and then cuts him or her in half with its huge teeth. I later learned hippos kill more humans in Africa than any other wild mammal.

The Nile originates from Lake Victoria in Uganda, passes through Sudan, then Egypt, and ends in the Mediterranean Sea. East Africa is highland, and when you go west toward South Sudan, it tilts lower. Once it comes to the plain, it widens. Right in the plain, when it's the dry season, the Nile shrinks. During the rainy season, the area around it is covered in floodwater. There were some places that didn't have water, and that was where we stayed.

Once we were on the island, we stayed for two days to rest and eat delicious fish and maize. Some people who had salt and extra clothing traded those for more maize that they could eat as we continued our journey on the other side of the river. After leaving the island, the fishermen showed those who were tall enough the route to wade across to the other side, while the children and those who were not were taken across in canoes. I took the canoe; little children couldn't wade, even though it was shallow for an adult. We had finally crossed the Nile.

From there we walked to the nearby Dinka Bor village called Baidit, also Mach Deng. It was so green. We saw herds of gazelles and antelopes, grazing by the hundreds on the plain. Baidit held rebel forces that had been attacking the government soldiers in the town of Bor, which was about twenty miles away. We did not go there. Like other towns we had left behind, it was under the government's control at that time. Baidit had a few buildings made of brick and zinc rooftops. Those buildings looked like schools, based on their design. There were villages around Baidit, but only SPLA soldiers lived in that small town.

Before South Sudan gained independence from the north, it was comprised of three provinces—Bhar el Ghazal, Equatoria, and the Upper Nile to which Bor belonged. Rumbek was located in Bhar el Ghazal. Baidit was in the Upper Nile province. The people who lived there, near the town of Bor, were Dinka Bor. That region was located in a vast swampy area that stretched miles away from the river and was heavily flooded when the Nile overflowed. There were no dense forests or the jungle. The vegetation consisted of scattered trees and wet grassland. You could see herds of deer, grazing in the distance.

The people of Baidit were very friendly and hospitable. We felt at home with them. They shared with us whatever they had, including quick-yield grains that they grew. They also provided us with milk and cows. After nothing but meat to eat that was a welcome change.

Even today, the Dinka in southern Sudan are pastoralists. The cow is so valuable. Owning cattle is everything to us; it is like having a bank account. We live on milk, making butter from it. Families use cows as dowries. Our people do not believe there is anything more important in the world than the cow.

The SPLA soldiers did not slaughter cows, as is our tradition, but instead shot them in the heads with their AK-47 rifles. Word went around among us that we were being given some cows, and soon I heard gunshots. *Pop! Pop!* The next thing I saw were cattle lying dead on the ground. I felt sad about the way they had been killed. Shooting a cow, to me, was too harsh and violent. The SPLA soldiers should have slaughtered them.

After they killed the cows, they called my uncle over to distribute them among the refugees. We, the children, always fought over cow tails. A boy who ran the fastest and touched the tail of a cow as soon as it fell dead to the ground got it, which the adults cooked. Before they prepared the tails, though, they put them over a fire to burn off the hair and then washed them. They cooked them in barrels—the rebel soldiers cut them into halves and used them for cooking—with the other meat so it could soak up the juices. It tasted good, like a pot roast.

After we left Baidit, we went directly to Kongor. We passed through Maar, Paliau, and Wanglei before reaching Kongor. All those little towns were a few hours' walk apart from one another. We stopped to cook and rest, but did not spend the night. The terrain was still the same, and mosquitoes were present, but there they did not swarm us like when we were at the Nile. I noticed something that these towns had in common. They all had many Neem trees. Neem trees don't grow very big. They're extremely green and produce bitter fruits smaller than grapes. The ravens like to eat them.

I saw ravens for the first time there. They perched in those trees in multitudes, ate tiny fruit, and made incessant noise. When I spotted them, I shouted to my uncle, "Look, Uncle, they have black crows around here." All I knew was a crow.

In Kongor, we met the commander of the SPLA, named Arok Thon. The day we arrived, he ordered people to bring six huge bulls and had soldiers shoot them. He was so happy that we had made it that far. After we ate and rested, he came and addressed us. He told us we would be all right if we could make it the rest of the way through Sudan to Ethiopia. We had made it seventy percent of the way. We were relieved to hear that. We supported the rebels. They protected us and gave us information on how to travel safely. We relied on the SPLA. They were black like us.

I did not feel resentment for the fighting. I witnessed the way things were with the government. They attacked us because we were black. I thought, even if the war had interrupted my schooling, I would be okay in the end because we would get our freedom one day. The handicapped would not be tortured. We'd have our own army that wouldn't kill and torture the innocent, and if there was a problem, they would fight army against rebel and they wouldn't harass civilians. We'd get our freedom. Ultimately, it would be worth it. I was very proud.

We stayed in Kongor for four days before we moved on. We passed through the small town of Warnyol and crossed the Jonglei Canal to Duk. The Jonglei Canal project was a plan designed by Sudan and Egypt as a way of channeling additional water from the Nile and all the wetlands and swamps in the south for use in northern Sudan and Egypt. The excavation started in 1978, but was never finished. The SPLA put a stop to the entire project in 1983.

If the government had finished the canal, it would have had enormously detrimental effects on the environment and local population and their livestock. People would have experienced a severe, even disastrous, shortage of water for their livestock and for themselves. The water from those swamps lasted throughout the dry season until the rainy season came again.

After crossing the canal, we arrived at Duk. The people of Duk, because they lived on the border with the Nuer and interacted with a neighboring tribe, the Nuer Lou, spoke a Dinka and Nuer dialect. The terrain changed. At the border between the Dinka and Nuer tribes, the wetland gradually changed to many scattered trees but was still wetland. The Nuer Lou people who lived there were tall and athletic like Dinkas. They owned livestock and grew crops as well.

The following day, we left Duk, and two hours later, we started to run into people from the Nuer Lou tribe. They were nice. We ran into another SPLA commander named Gatwich, who happened to be from Nuer. He addressed us in the same manner as Commander Thon had in Kongor. He said we were close to the Ethiopian border, but warned us that we had a tough desert ahead to cross.

I was so relieved and excited to hear that we were close to Ethiopia, but as soon as Commander Gatwich warned us about the desert, I started to worry. Gatwich told us to relax and rest. He said we needed a lot of energy to be able to beat the Akobo Desert. We did as he instructed and ate, slept, and just relaxed. We stayed there for about ten days. We had better food and lots of milk to drink. The SPLA soldiers killed many gazelles and provided us with meat. Finally, we had to leave.

Chapter 8

Crossing the Sahara Akobo Desert

At six p.m. we set out for the Sahara Akobo, which is a semi-arid desert. Even though we were cutting through the edge of it on the way out of Sudan to Ethiopia, it took us eighteen hours to cross, from six p.m. until noon the next day. There was no water in the desert, so we carried small Jerry cans full of it.

My uncle kept pushing me to move faster, faster, always faster. Every now and then, we encountered human skeletons along the way. I was scared after I saw those remains and that motivated me to walk even faster. I did not want to be left behind and end up like those whose bones were scattered along the trail.

When someone in our group sat to rest, we knew they were done. Those who became too exhausted to walk anymore were left behind. That was the end of their lives there. Nobody could carry anybody. Everyone was just trying to save his or her own life.

In the desert, there was no hope, and you can't help anybody. You wanted to, but you if you did, then both of you would die.

Later, I was reminded of this when I watched the devastation that people in New Orleans experienced when hurricane Katrina hit. Families were split. Some people just died in their houses.

By 11:30 in the morning, we saw a bunch of thick green trees in the distance. That meant we approached the Akobo River and the desert was about to end. We noticed tall, green grass as well. We knew there must be water around. Where there was tall, green grass there must be water. We were greatly relieved and fired up. Everyone started picking up the pace, trying to get there as soon as possible. I do not know where that last gasp of energy originated from; I guess it came from wanting to find out whether there was water ahead of us. Even the people who lagged behind caught up with the whole group.

It was a beautiful scene. The green vegetation reminded me of the Nile environment. Fifteen minutes later, a cool breeze welcomed us. I enjoyed that fresh air like a cow enjoying the cool breeze of the first rain during the rainy season.

At noon, we arrived at the river. We plunged into the water and drank like a herd of thirsty cattle. The water was fresher and cleaner than the Nile's. The Akobo/Sobat River is narrower than the Nile, but its current is much stronger. After we finished drinking and bathing, exhausted from the ordeal of the desert, we slept under the trees alongside the river to regain our strength. The local people offered us grain that we boiled and ate. They provided us with milk as well. Despite the fact that Tirgol, the SPLA base, was only about half an hour away on the other side of the river, we decided to rest first.

Around four p.m. the local people of Nuer Lou ferried us across the river, and by 4:30 we arrived in Tirgol, which was very close to Akobo and had many SPLA soldiers. Akobo was a few miles away; only the river separated it from Tirgol.

The SPLA soldiers in Tirgol had dug trenches all around the base in case of shelling or air strikes from government forces. The SPLA had artillery and other heavy weapons such as large machine guns.

Upon our arrival, we were told to stay under trees and not to move about. If too many people roamed around the base, a government warplane might spot us and drop bombs. Without the SPLA, nobody would have made it out of Sudan. They protected refugees fleeing the war.

Unfortunately, at three p.m. the following day, the government had heard the news of new refugees in Tirgol. We were cooking under a tree, boiling corn, when the government forces shelled us. The first mortar shell fell and killed three people before they could make it to a trench. As we ran, the rebel soldiers blew whistles, indicating an emergency. Some people didn't make it to the trenches and died. It brought me back to the moment of the shelling at the water pump. It was the same sound, like a tree branch snapping. The explosions smelled like gasoline.

The SPLA could tell the government soldiers shelled us with 120 mm mortars, which always reached Tirgol. The SPLA soldiers did not respond. If they did, the fighting would escalate and as a result put more refugees at risk. The shelling stopped after about a half an hour. Luckily, there were not any air raids while we were there.

Later that night, on the advice of the SPLA commander, we were told to leave for Itang the following morning. The SPLA commander was concerned for our safety on the front line of battle. He sent for Mangar to come to his headquarters to work out with him the route to the Itang refugee camp in Ethiopia. Our plan had been to stay in Tirgol for a week to rest because we were exhausted after crossing the desert. We had bruises and swelling on our feet, but fear of government attack compelled our leaders to get us out of there as quickly as possible.

My uncle came back, and said, "Ater, we are leaving tomorrow morning for Itang."

I said to him, "You told us that we would stay here for a while. Why are you changing your mind now? I am very tired. We should stay here for at least three days."

He insisted, "Our safety is uncertain here. Itang is only seven days away from here. We have to leave."

Fortunately, later that night while I was sleeping, Mangar was told to cancel the departure. I went to sleep knowing we were going to leave in the morning, but when I woke up Mangar said, "We are not leaving today." I could not believe him. I thought he was joking, but he kept saying, "We are not leaving." I was relieved. That meant my bruises and the swelling in my feet would have enough time to heal.

A short time later, my uncle surprised me with even better news. He said, "We are not going to walk to Itang on foot. A helicopter will come from Ethiopia and fly everybody to Itang." That meant no more walking and no more mosquitoes or the constant danger of being killed by government soldiers either.

I was ecstatic. Now, I would get to fly for the first time. I wanted to see how the ground and trees looked from the air. It was late June at that time, and rain was heavy, flooding everywhere. The water was as high as peoples' waists in some places. The route to Itang was heavily flooded and too difficult to cover on foot. The United Nations Refugee Agency, UNHCR, learned of our arrival at the Sudan-Ethiopian border, the security concern, and the road conditions, and they decided to send helicopters to transport us to the Itang refugee camp.

The same day we had been planning to leave on foot, two helicopters came and picked us up at around two p.m., and continued doing so until all the refugees were flown to Itang. First, they transported children and then adults. On the helicopter, we sat on the floor because there were no seats. It really did not matter to me. It was much, much better than walking. In the beginning, when the helicopter took off, my stomach moved up and down in a weird way. Because of the takeoff, many children threw up. Once we reached a higher altitude, my stomach calmed down.

We were able to see through small windows. From above, the vegetation looked so green and beautiful. I believe the pilot must have enjoyed showing us the sights. Whenever he saw animals in a clearing, he flew lower so we could take a good look at them. One time he went low and we crossed over giraffes running across the plain below.

Before reaching Itang, we saw the Ethiopian mountains in the distance. At first, we thought they were dark clouds. Someone shouted, "Look at those big clouds. It probably rains a lot where we are going." As we came closer and closer, it became clear that they were not clouds. None of us had ever seen a mountain firsthand, only in pictures. Where I grew up, there weren't any at all, only big trees.

The flight from Tirgol to Itang took about forty-five minutes. At a distance, the camp looked like herds of cattle, grazing on the plain. Everybody was curious to make sense of what we saw. An Ethiopian man in the helicopter with us said simply, "Itang, Itang."

Chapter 9

Itang Refugee Camp

The Itang refugee camp, near Gambela in western Ethiopia, was filled with thousands of refugees like me who had fled Sudan.

As the helicopter came closer and closer, the tents kept getting bigger and bigger. I was relieved and excited, but still could not believe our journey was ending until the aircraft touched down on small airstrip in the middle of the camp. A large number of people were standing along the sides, waiting.

The helicopter landed. I got out, but I did not see anyone I knew. My uncle was still in Tirgol. Because he was a leader, he had to come last. Right after we climbed off the helicopter, we were taken to the UNHCR, United Nation High Commissioner for the Refugee, compound to get us registered as refugees. Ethiopians were employed there. They talked to us through translators about how to meet basic needs such as food and finding drinking water.

Being officially registered by the UNHCR as a refugee was a big relief to me and the others; that meant we no longer had to fear government troops, mortar rounds exploding among us, or having to flee war that indisciminantly killed many civilians, including old people, women, and children. We were safe from war, at least for the time being. Now began the effort to simply survive.

My second cousin, Kedit Madol, who was probably twenty years old then, walked around, looking among newly arrived refugees, seeing if there was anyone he knew. When he saw me, he said, "Hey! Who is this guy who looks like Ater? Is that you, Ater?"

I said, "It's me!"

Kedit and me in Juba, South Sudan in February, 2017

He almost wept when he realized it was me, amazed that I had made it out alive. He barely recognized me as I had become very skinny, badly malnourished. He told me, "Go ahead and get registered so you can get food and supplies."

Once registered, we were given new clothes to replace our ragged clothing and tents. We were given food, sugar, salt, milk, and many other things for which we were very grateful. I only wish they had given us shoes.

After registration, he took me home to his place, and I had a shower and he gave me clothing and shoes. I felt very good. Then he took me around, and I met some other relatives who were in the camp. It felt almost like being at home. I met my cousin, Mayek Marial. His dad and my dad are brothers. I also met one of the big boys who used to hunt with me named Nyangkot Dut and many friends.

Dut told Kedit, "Please let Ater hang out with me for a while. This is my boy. I missed him a lot."

Kedit agreed, and said: "You guys should hang out for a while, but I will come back later and get him." He left.

Dut prepared a meal that consisted of beans and starch called assida. It is made with boiled water and flour. When it is cooked, it looks like mashed potatoes. You can eat it with cooked beans, milk, meat, okra, or any vegetable. In Kenya, it is called ugali. It is similar to grits, except it's thicker. It is somewhat tasteless.

After we ate, we talked about all kinds of stuff, especially stories about when we used to hunt. In Rumbek, hunting was one of my favorite activities. We roamed miles away from home and hunted deer and dik-dik gazelles. Once we located them, the dogs ran them down. We used bows and arrows or clubs. I had a male hunting dog named Machakel, which means "problems" in Arabic. He brought home a female hunting dog we named Nyilok, which means dark gray. Both dogs loved to hunt.

Most of the time they caught one or two animals; rarely, they caught nothing. My main job was to carry the meat and bring my dogs because I was there to learn since I was too small for the action. When it was time to cook, I made the fire.

One time I was hunting with Matenh and the dogs spotted a cheetah and ran after it. All I had was a club that was about two feet long. I was the smallest of the boys at that time and was trying to keep up. The cheetah disappeared, and suddenly I saw it running toward me and it jumped at me to my right. I did not even know what to do so I just swung the club and hit it on the nostril.

The cheetah fell onto the ground and was about to get up when the dogs arrived just in time. They ganged up on it and killed it. Matenh chased them away after he made sure the cheetah was dead. He did not want the dogs to tear the hide to pieces. Matenh singled me out from all the boys on the hunt by saying, "Ater, this hide is yours because you were the first person to hit the cheetah." That was the first hide I had ever earned in such a way. My dad sold it for a goat that we used for milk and to breed more goats. Young people buy cheetah hides, which are very valuable, and they use them for traditional dancing.

After we told stories, Dut said, "Ater, I would like you to live with me, but I really do not know if Kedit, your cousin, would agree to that."

I replied, "Dut, there are no worries. Since we are going to live close to one another, we can still hang out on a daily basis. I am glad to have made it here."

A few hours later, Kedit came back to get me. He said, "Ater, I hope you had a good time with Dut. Now, we should go home."

I said, "Yes, we had fun." We said goodbye to Dut and left.

Kedit was living with three other adults and a boy named Dak Aggrey, who all had kinship with me. In our culture, we can trace our ancestors up to thirteen generations. That process allows us to avoid marrying people who are related to us. Unlike Dut, who lived in a tent, Kedit had two thatched houses. Once my Uncle Mangar arrived at the camp, he lived with adults in a tent. He told me that I should live with Kedit since he had a better place to stay. I still visited my uncle.

The Itang Refugee Camp was located in a muddy area near the river, the same one that runs all the way to Sudan and becomes the Akobo River. Thousands of refugees, many of them starving when they arrived, continued to pour into the camp, escaping the violence and genocidal attacks by the Sudanese government.

Although we had escaped war, life in the camp continued to be a struggle. The rainy season was particularly dreary, with mud everywhere. Cars and trucks stayed on the main road because if they went off it they became stuck. When it rained, water pooled until it rained again and everywhere you walked it was deep in mud. People often dispensed with shoes to better navigate the deep mud and to protect their footwear. If a person slipped and fell, people would mock that person in a goodnatured way by saying, "Oh, awel, awel." Awel means "turn him, turn him" in Dinka; when a person fell, he or she rolled around in the mud. Those were moments of fun to break the monotony of the camp. During the rainy season, there were few opportunities for recreation, except for tribal dances on Sundays on the airstrip when breaks came in the incessant rainfall.

Itang became considerably more active during the dry season. Kids played all sorts of games outdoors, and adults wore nicer clothing and shoes and walked freely in the camp. People played soccer and volleyball. Others went to the river and swam. I enjoyed playing soccer, and Aggrey taught me how to swim. During the rainy season, nobody swam in the river because crocodiles were more prevalent then.

The UNHCR brought us corn, beans, powdered milk, cooking oil, butter, and sugar. There were two flour mills in the whole camp. Once we received our food ration, we took the corn to the flour mill to get it ground. Then we could make assida/ugali that we ate with either cooked beans or milk. We mixed the powdered milk with water before eating assida/ugali with it.

The UNHCR did not provide us with fruits, vegetables, or meat. If refugees wanted to get any of those foods, they had to sell some of their own rations in the local markets for money and then in turn use that to purchase meat, fish, or vegetables. The local people of Anyuak brought all kinds of items to the markets.

Some people, especially young men, worked as porters to unload UNHCR trucks that brought food rations to the refugees. As a result, they were paid with sacks of corn that they sold to buy meat in the market. Others walked miles to the forest to gather firewood and then sold it in order to buy missing necessities.

As the demand for firewood increased rapidly, people turned to cutting down trees to sell, which created major deforestation in an area that was already lacking trees. Before too long the vicinity of Itang looked semiarid. People cut down trees, chopped them into short logs that were manageable, and then split them little by little into thin logs. They dried those for days and then sold them as firewood in the market. Some women made liquor from corn and sold it.

In our household, however, we did not sell our food rations or pick firewood because my cousin, Kedit, was employed as one of the leaders in the camp. All the leaders were paid with sacks of corn. When Kedit sold it and gave us money, Dak Aggrey and I went to buy fish, meat, or vegetables, whenever we needed a change of diet. Since we were the only boys and did not have anything to do, we cooked for everybody in the house. Cooking was the only way we could contribute.

Kedit told us that we were lucky to have arrived after the UNHCR had improved the camp. When they had first arrived in 1984, life was bad. Many people died from diarrhea. There were no latrines. People defecated in the open, and when the rain came, it washed all the feces into the river that they drank from. Imagine thousands of people going out in the open and defecating every day. That was really a cause for an epidemic.

Kedit said there was a metal-like substance in the water that sickened people as well. Once they got the water from the river, they had to boil it first, allow it to sit for a while so that substance sank, and then pour the water into a different container and leave some in there with all the impurities. Those who did not take time to go through that process sometimes died from drinking the water. He also told us that they did not have flour mills then. So they pounded the corn to produce flour to make a meal.

Fortunately, when we arrived in Itang, in July 1985, everything was in place. We had flour mills, so we did not have to pound the corn. Because of the diseases that those who came before us, like Kedit Madol, contracted from drinking water, the UNHCR set up a water purification system by the river. They brought huge containers that were several times the size of cargo ones and they filled these with purified water three times a day. They also instructed refugee leaders to tell people to dig latrines and not to defecate in the open because that was what caused the epidemic of diarrhea. I was so glad we did not have to experience what they had gone through.

Chapter 10

Dimma Refugee Camp. Not Enough Cookies

As the number of refugees increased, other refugee camps were established, such as Dimma and Panyudo, to avoid overpopulation in Itang. According to media reports, the Itang refugee camp, the largest of several camps along the Ethiopian border, at one point swelled to nearly 200,000 refugees.

In the fall of 1986, about 1,000 children, including myself, were moved from Itang refugee camp to Dimma refugee camp in southwestern Ethiopia. Dimma is near the border of southern Sudan and Kenya.

My Uncle Mangar and I were separated. Young children, including me—I was ten years old then—who couldn't go to war and fight were moved to Dimma where we attended makeshift school taught by other refugees. Young men who were older, eighteen plus, joined the SPLA and went to war to fight the government of Sudan. My uncle was trained as an SPLA soldier; since 1986, he'd been fighting as a soldier. He started as a second lieutenant and eventually rose to general, commanding a brigade at the northern border.

We were told the reason we were being moved was mainly for educational purposes and that Dimma was better than Itang for several reasons. First, it was situated in a hilly area, so when it rained, it did not get as muddy as Itang. At Dimma, the water ran off into a creek that was alongside the camp. We were also informed that once we arrived there, the

UNHCR would provide us with school materials, such as pens, pencils, textbooks, and so on and that we were going to focus on schooling. Based on what we were being told, the benefits of going to Dimma outweighed staying in Itang, even though we didn't have a choice of whether or not to go. I was excited to leave nasty, muddy Itang. Once they mentioned we were going to Dimma, they said we'd get our own section of the refugee camp to work on education. What got us so excited was the fact that we were going to be students again.

We were organized into groups. If you had been put into a particular group, you didn't have any other option to move to one that you would prefer. All the children who were in the camp that year were moved to Dimma. Our leaders stressed that there were more than 5,000 refugees there, so we were not going to miss Itang that much. They told us Dimma was the second biggest camp to Itang.

We were told that we were going to travel on foot along the Sudan-Ethiopia border until we got to Dimma refugee camp. They couldn't get us cars; I don't know why. They provided us with four days of food rations because that was how long the trip would take when walking. We had to carry it on our heads since our bedding was in our backpacks. We set off traveling through Anyuak tribe territory. The Anyuak are Sudanese, but those who live in Ethiopian territory consider themselves Ethiopians geographically.

We traveled through that territory at a slow pace. Those who were very young could not carry heavier weight, and their portions had to be distributed among those who were older, such as youth aged fifteen, sixteen, or seventeen. However, the younger children carried their own bedding plus cooking utensils.

We did not face any threats. The Anyuak is a peaceful tribe. They are not aggressive. They only fight in self-defense. We had leaders, grown-ups, who led us all the way with the help of local people. We walked for about six or seven hours a day and then rested at a village. If we wanted some fruit or vegetables, we traded whatever we had with the Anyuak. Mostly, they needed salt.

Their land is extremely fertile. They grow bananas and mangos, sweet potatoes, yams, and corn. They are not pastoralists like the Dinka, but they did own chickens and dogs. They also liked to fish and hunt. They lived in clusters, not like the Dinka, who live spread out.

Once we finally arrived at the Dimma refugee camp, we had several surprises. First, it did not initially appear that there were many refugees. We found a few thatched houses and tents scattered all over the hillsides.

The UNHCR compound was very small relative to the one in Itang—it consisted of a few tents erected on the top of a hill. We went to the compound and were registered.

While we stood in a queue, one of the UNHCR personnel handed out biscuits, cookies. In the beginning, it was orderly. We were in a long, straight line, but then they announced they had run out of cookies. On hearing that, those who didn't get any attacked other kids who had gotten some. It was a disorderly mess. The UNHCR tent was knocked over in the melee, so the UNHCR officials had to close down the registration that day and told everybody to leave. I got a cookie, but the moment I saw other children being attacked, I ran as fast I could down the hill. One boy tried to run after me, but I outran him.

At that point, I realized the camp was in the early stages of organization. When we had left Itang, we were told we were going to a large, established camp, but it wasn't true. We arrived in December, and it had only been set up earlier that year, so it wasn't big. There were fewer than 3,000 people at the time of our arrival. Basically, we were starting the camp from scratch.

I believe we were moved to Dimma to provide a more convenient center from which to distribute aid. In addition, refugees from the eastern Equatorial province in southern Sudan could more easily get there and did not have to walk all the way to the more northern Itang.

In the beginning, life was extremely difficult. The UNHCR provided us with corn, beans, and cooking oil, but there were no flour mills to grind the corn.

We went to the hillsides and picked up large flat rocks. We used an iron or a small rock to smooth out the top of the rocks. Finally, we poured a few corns on the flat surface and used another round rock, about five pounds, to crush the corn. After getting sufficient flour, we cooked assida, which is starch made from boiled water and flour, which we ate with cooked pinto beans.

Grinding stone

 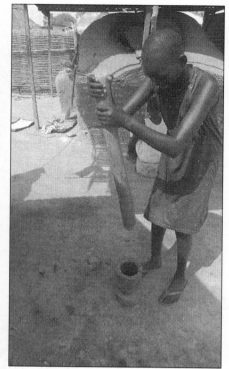

Pounding grain into flour

Grinding corn on a rock in that manner to produce enough flour for a meal for a group of ten was timeconsuming and hard labor. You had to sit for about two to three hours to get about a gallon of flour. As a result, we turned to what our mothers used to do to make enough—an improvised mortar and pestle.

We went and cut thick logs and carved the insides out, and then cut long, thick branches to use as pestles. They were just like the small mortars and pestles that people used with one hand to grind stuff like garlic, except we magnified them. We made them much bigger so we could pound enough corn. We would pour about a gallon of corn at a time and then two people would alternately pound it until it produced some flour. Then we would take that batch out and use a sieve to separate the flour from the grain. We put the corn that had not been well-pounded back into the mortar and pounded it again and again until we got an adequate amount to make a meal.

A group was comprised of ten people, but we ate in fives. We would assign two people to cook for the whole group. That way, once you were done with your turn, you'd have four days before cooking again. Once on duty, it was up to the individuals cooking to figure out how to go about doing it.

Whenever I was on duty, I suggested to my partner that we divide the chores. One person went to the forest to collect firewood while the other pounded the corn. Once he came back from fetching the firewood, we both finished pounding the corn. We cooked the beans while doing that. It was very hard work. I didn't like it. Our palms became scaly and rough as a result. I had no choice but to do it, though. The UNHCR really should have brought us flour mills.

Another thing that troubled us very much was a lack of shoes. Most of us didn't have any. The UNHCR did not provide refugees with them, only food. Itang was better. We could sell some of our food rations for money. However, at Dimma, we couldn't do that. The local people of the Kachipo tribe—people who make big holes in their lips—lived in the mountains nearby and were so poor they couldn't afford to buy our corn. They begged us for food.

There was a tick called tuktuk, which hung out under the trees where we had makeshift classes. This insect penetrated our feet, sucked our blood, and grew to the size of a maggot. Some children were not able to walk due to the wounds caused by that tick. Even if someone had shoes, whenever she or he took them off at night, the tick got into them and eventually into his or her feet. We went to the creek to soak them, and sit by the riverside and use needles to get these ticks out. It was excruciating. Sometimes, once having gotten the tick out, the wound bleed right away.

When we first arrived in Dimma, we temporarily stayed in the actual camp, for about a month. After that, we were moved to about a fifteen-minute walk away from the refugee center. Refugee leaders chose a flat area along the creek. We were told to build our own thatched houses there. We were provided with sickles with which to mow the grass. In the morning, we were sent far away to cut it and carry it home on our heads. It was hot work, and I recall sweating profusely under the blazing sun. The sand scorched our bare feet and, with the weight of big bundles of grass on our heads, we had to keep pushing ourselves ahead until we got home. We cut wood and designed our own houses. We made them like dormitories. Each dorm had a capacity of fifty students.

We were told not to sleep on the dirt floor because of fear that insects, including the ticks, might get into our ears while sleeping. Therefore, we went to the forest, cut wood, and made our own improvised beds. We put down wood first, then some grass and tied it down with strings. After everything was firm and tight, we spread sheets of canvas on them to make them feel soft and comfortable. They were from our old tents that we had lived in when we had first arrived in Dimma. After we built those dorms, we didn't need to sleep in tents anymore. We cut them into sheets that perfectly fit the beds. Canvas tents were preferable in areas where it rained a lot because of their waterproof quality. The beds we made weren't as comfortable as regular mattresses, but they were suitable for that environment. We also made tables and seats with wood. It was a lot of hard work.

Chapter 11

Back to School

It wasn't all work in Dimma. I was a child, and along with the other children, found ways to play. In the beginning, we didn't have a soccer ball, but created a makeshift one. We took an old torn-up sock and stuffed many other old socks into it until it became firm and solid and then used it to play with during our break times.

Every Sunday, refugees performed tribal dances in Dimma's center. We all got as dressed up as we could to attend them. It was very interesting and exciting, because we were able to see different types of dances. For instance, I watched ones from Lotuko, Dinka Agar, and Toposa.

In the Lotuko dance, the dancers formed two circles. The outer one was comprised of men, and the inner of girls. In the center, there was a drummer and a horn blower. It wasn't a real horn, but an improvised one—made of something like bamboo. They hollowed it out to blow through. It was about two meters long. The interesting thing about it was the beautiful, unique rumbling sound it produced. Men took their shirts off and then sprinkled ashes on their chests and backs. I didn't know the significance of it, but it was pleasant to look at it anyway. Women wore beautifully adorned outfits. The drum, horn, women, and men singing all took place at the same time. That blend of different sounds and voices created magnificent polyrhythmic beats that captivated the senses.

My clan dance, Dinka Agar, was very distinctive from others. The dancers formed one big circle. Half of it was made up of men, and the other was comprised of girls. The guy who beat the drum stayed outside the circle. The men clapped and sang. The girls did neither of those things. Once the dance started, a girl chosed a fellow to dance with either by stepping on his foot or pointing at him. The guy jumped into the air as high as he could while chasing the girl around in the circle. The girl raised her hands high as if she pushed something upward and then danced while moving backward and facing the guy in front of her. After she was done dancing, it was another girl's turn to choose who she wanted to dance with.

People made fun of guys who didn't jump very high. There was this one very tall fellow—I'd guess about seven feet—who jumped so high his feet reached about half a meter above the ground. He was such an impressive dancer, and entertained everybody. That dance was exciting to watch when there were guys who jumped very high; otherwise it could be somewhat boring.

Lotuko's dance was probably the most consistent. Every time was the same and it was interesting, the way people danced, the way they moved. These dances were the only events that went on over the course of the week, so we patiently waited for them.

After we had built our dorms, we were told the school would be along the creek under the trees. So we cut logs and made benches under them by the stream. Even though we had experienced hardship, I was excited to be back in school once again. Those who were teachers in Sudan before becoming refugees volunteered to teach us along with people from other occupations—including older students or those who had worked for the government in Sudan.

Whoever came up with the decision to move us to Dimma had made an incredible impact on our lives. That school helped a lot of children. I started learning English there, under those trees.

We were very focused on school. I guess maybe that was why they had moved us away from the actual refugee camp so we wouldn't be distracted. School took place from Monday to Friday. We started classes at around eight a.m. and ended at two p.m. Being back in school was something I really enjoyed very much. I never thought I'd get the opportunity to do so, and be able to sit in a classroom once again. Despite the fact we attended makeshift school, taught under trees, we were very happy to be learning.

When war broke out in Rumbek, I despaired, feeling my aspiration for an education was shattered. My dream was to go to a university and become a medical doctor, something my dad hadn't accomplished because he went to school late in his life. Being back in class, those memories creeped into my mind. At that point, though, it didn't matter whether I became a doctor or not. My main goal in the refugee school was to learn English.

Even though I had been in an Arabic school, my dad had insisted on teaching me English. I remember Dad saying, "Ater, I have a feeling that in the future, English will be the official language of Sudan. This Arabic of yours won't do you any good." My dad taught me the English alphabet back home in Sudan and had started teaching me how to read in a book called *A Man and a Pan*.

Once fellow refugees taught me English, I remembered what my father had told me. From that point on, I felt strongly that the Sudan People's Liberation Army, SPLA, was fighting for ordinary citizens like me. Our teachers told us that we were going to be the seeds for a new Sudan. They said, "The education that you get under these trees is not going to be different from the one somebody got in the classroom. We are still in the bush, even though we sleep in these thatched houses. Hardship will make you stronger. Even with the pounding of the corn, ticks penetrating your feet and sucking your blood, and everything attacking you from left to right, all you should be doing is focusing on your homework and learning something. Someday these hardships will pay off."

We were whipped for coming to school late. In our culture, teachers have the right to whip students. We don't consider it abuse or oppression on their part, but as a way of showing us the right path in life. The teachers deserved the respect we gave to our parents or elders. Therefore, whatever they told us or did to us, we took it for granted as something beneficial for us. We regarded them as our mentors, not just our teachers.

In the beginning, most of our teachers were volunteers. However, later on, when the UNHCR found out that most people were genuinely interested in educating children, they hired the number of teachers needed and paid them salaries. Originally, we started it as a community thing. Even when the UNHCR registered a certain number of teachers who were required to cover classes and get paid on a monthly basis, there were still so many people who continued to volunteer. We had plenty of willing human resources.

On a daily basis, we were busy with schoolwork. Whenever school started, everyone focused on doing homework instead of hanging out with friends. We took it as seriously as children in the United States and the rest of the world, maybe more so because it meant so much to us.

From 1987 through 1988, an influx of new refugees, including many children, showed up in Dimma. As a result, I met boys who I had known from back home, including Manyank Kau, Makwac Aggrey, a former classmate, and Matong Wilson Mabor. I hung out with those people. At that time, Dimma became much more interesting. We played cards and went swimming in the stream. We also played soccer because by then the UNHCR had brought us actual soccer balls. There weren't big matches, relative to the ones we used to have in Itang since Dimma was much smaller.

That same year, Amuna John, the cousin of my dad, showed up with her husband. They made their own thatch house in the center of Dimma. The arrival of Amuna changed my life tremendously. Because we were children, way out there in the student center, we were isolated from the main camp. We'd just get our rations. We didn't have the resources to sell them. The people in the main camp could send someone to Aman, an Ethiopian town, where they'd buy all kinds of stuff, and the women cooked anything that was bought. We, the little children in the camp, all we got were corn and beans. There was no extra food, and no one allowed us to rent a car and travel to the city.

Amuna cooked food similar to what my mom used to cook me back in Rumbek. She said, "Ater, don't keep yourself in the children's camp where you eat the same monotonous beans and starch every day. Don't you get sick and tired of eating the same thing? You should at least come to our house and have dinner with us sometimes."

So, two to three times a week, whenever I needed a change of diet, I took Amuna up on her offer to eat with them. Besides food, I enjoyed talking about home. Just being able to a have a conversation with someone related to me was very comforting, more than anything else.

Because of the lack of protein in our diet, some children made nets and used them to catch fish in the creek. A young man named Ngong Akuei, who belonged to my group, took us fishing and we caught many fish.

During the summer, we hung out in the moonlight until almost two in the morning. We took turns telling stories. Ngong Akuei, in particular, was a compelling storyteller. I remember one he told about a young relative who belonged to a gang in Khartoum back in the mid-1970s. He said whenever there was a power outage, his relative and gang members climbed walls and robbed houses at gunpoint. When we asked him why his relative did such horrible things to innocent people, he justified it by saying, "Most children didn't have jobs, so they had to do whatever they could to survive."

Wherever Ngong Akuei was, a bunch of people gathered, eager to listen to his engaging stories. We also told folktales. For example, when we were little kids, on a clear, starry night, we said it was the fox herding the cows that day. The stars represented cows. Because so many were visible, it was the fox that herded them because the fox doesn't eat cows. When there were fewer scattered stars, we assumed it was the hyena's turn because it kept eating cows while they grazed.

We talked about things back home, whether there had been enough rain and local farmers had good harvests. Mostly we talked about the SPLA's progress on the war front. We were very interested in the success of the SPLA—if they were successful, perhaps we could go back home. Under trees or in the dorm, we discussed whether the SPLA could liberate Sudan so we could return, or whether we were going to end up staying in the refugee camp indefinitely if the movement didn't succeed. Most of the time, we stayed positive. We didn't dwell on the negative for long.

John Garang, the SPLA leader, claimed he wanted to liberate the whole of Sudan, not just the south. Looking at the country on the map, we didn't see any possibility that the SPLA could fight all the way to the capital, Khartoum. The Sudanese Army was well-armed because of their oil resources, and the SPLA was poorly equipped. We also talked about unity within the movement itself. If the SPLA stayed cohesive as a unit, we knew we could succeed.

Every day, from three p.m. to four p.m., we sat in the shade under the trees with shortwave radios, listening to the Voice of SPLA—a news broadcast by the Sudan People's Liberation Army. The government of Ethiopia provided the SPLA with a radio station in Addis Ababa, the Ethiopian capital, where the SPLA broadcasted their news, mostly developments on the war front. Day after day in 1989, we heard of the SPLA's victory after victory. They had destroyed an enemy convoy, brought down a plane, or captured a town. Sometimes, the SPLA leader, Dr. Garang, addressed the nation using the Voice of the SPLA, and everybody in the camps and around the country listened to his speeches. He emphasized the importance of education for all the children in the refugee camps and those in the diaspora. He believed the children in all the camps and those pursuing education overseas were the future of Sudan.

All the SPLA leaders, including Garang, stressed that the children in the refugee camps were the seeds of a new Sudan. They wanted us to pursue education so we would be able to serve the country after they had liberated it. I think that was why we were placed in school in Dimma. I breezed through grades one and two and passed the tests, so I was promoted to grade three. We did four years of school in Dimma, from 1987 until the fall of Ethiopia in May 1991.

Chapter 12

The Fall of the Ethiopian Government

In 1983, when the SPLA took up arms and rebelled in Southern Sudan, the first place they went to for sanctuary and as a base of operations was Ethiopia. Mengistu Haile Mariam had been the president of Ethiopia since 1974, when he had participated in the overthrow of Emperor Haile Selassie. Mengistu was friends with Garang, the leader of the SPLA. The relationship between Mengistu and Garang dated as far back as 1983, when no other country had recognized the Southern Sudanese struggle for their freedom, except Ethiopia. Mengistu hosted Sudanese refugees and provided military training for the SPLA as they struggled to achieve the liberation of South Sudan.

Mengistu had rebellion within his own country. Back then, Eritrea and Ethiopia were one nation, but Eritrea fought to obtain their independence. Other rebel groups also opposed Mengistu, who ruled his country like a dictator; many people were killed during his regime. Sudan's government had supported the rebels fighting against the government of Ethiopia as early as 1980. Three rebel groups—Oromo Liberation Front, OLF, Gambela People's Liberation Front, GPLF, and the Eritrean People's Liberation Front, EPLF—all were based in Sudan.

In 1991, the Ethiopian rebels were very effective in capturing many towns in Ethiopia. Mengistu's government eventually collapsed. Since the new government of Ethiopia had close ties with Sudan's government, there was a general belief among the SPLA leadership and refugees that the Sudanese Army might launch an attack on the SPLA through Ethiopian territory.[12]

Mengistu consulted with Garang and the SLPA leadership to make sure the refugees were moved out of Ethiopia. Because of the inability of the SPLA to initiate diplomatic talks with Ethiopian rebel groups, there was a rapid evacuation of the SPLA camps and personnel from Ethiopia. Refugees were afraid of what the new Ethiopian government might do. Since the Ethiopian rebels sided with the Sudanese government, our security likely was threatened. That was why the SPLA leadership told everyone to leave. They organized a mass evacuation of the Itang, Panyudo, and Dimma camps.

Some refugees initially did not heed the evacuation order to go back to Sudan, which later forced some SLPA forces to Ethiopia, just to make sure the refugees were safe. The Ethiopian government wanted the SPLA out and said only the refugees could stay, but the SLPA did not trust that. Some people in the new Ethiopian government hated the South Sudanese.

Because of the threat posed, the SPLA leadership also had to evacuate most of its personnel along with all the refugee camps. The refugees from Panyudo went to Pochalla, a SPLA-held town, while those from Dimma went to Pakok, a SPLA outpost near Boma. One-third of the Itang refugee camp went through Nasir, because the majority of Itang's population was of the Nuer ethnic group. It was convenient for them to do so since the Nuer's homes are located in that region. However, some of the Dinkas and other tribes from Equatoria, whose residents were farther away, joined with the refugees from Panyudo and went to Pochalla.

---

12   Douglas Johnson, *The Root Causes of Sudan's Civil Wars* (Bloomington: Indiana University Press, 2003), 88

In Dimma, the evacuation began with the communities, women and children, and then minors. People left Dimma peacefully in the first week of June 1991. Women and their kids left on June 1st followed by minors on June 7th. The journey from Dimma to Pakok in the Sudan-Ethiopian border lasted a couple of days, about seventeen hours. Before Pakok, though, we had to pass through dozens of SPLA outposts along the road from Dimma to Boma, SPLA-held towns. From Dimma, we passed through Kordengmajok, Korramala, Koradeed, Koranyuak, Jebel Rhad, Pakok, and then Boma.

The journey was at a slow pace. We carried food on our heads and bedding on our backs. Besides the heavy loads, such lengthy walking was something new. We had been in the refugee camps for several years without having to walk such a long distance. Furthermore, we were young, and the terrain was rugged and hilly from Dimma all the way to Boma. I was sixteen years old.

Most of us did not have shoes, including myself, when we covered this brutal, rugged gravel road, making walking seem like a snail's pace. We had bruises on our feet caused by being barefoot on gravel, and we were sore all over our bodies from going up steep hills. The walking time between the SPLA outposts we passed through was approximately three to four hours on average.

On top of those hardships, there was continual rain. Every night we became drenched. We had no shelter. We used blankets to cover ourselves, but they were quickly saturated. When the morning dawned, we squeezed the rainwater out of them and let them dry.

The SPLA outposts we passed by were very small and, when there was rain, did not have enough shelter to accommodate even a small fraction of all the traveling returnees. Some outposts had a few thatched huts in which a small number of soldiers lived and guarded military supplies, mostly ammunition. There were no houses whatsoever in those outposts. Besides, our number was so large that even sitting in the compound areas did not suffice. As a result, we slept on the grass and ground in the area around the outposts. In the mornings, when we left, we looked back and saw all the grass and small shrubs where we had slept were crushed flat as a parking lot.

Once we arrived in Pakok, our lives continued to be a grim and desperate struggle for survival. We were starving. There was little food after we had exhausted what we carried on our heads. We survived by eating leaves and roots of trees. The SPLA provided groups of 200 people with one cow for three days. With that kind of food shortage, people ate every part of the cow, including the skin. The only parts we didn't consume were inedible ones, such as horns and hooves. We ate the skin, legs, and the head for a day and the rest of the cow for the other two days. There was no such thing as breakfast, lunch, or dinner. We ate once a day. We had to cook in the middle of the day to divide the twenty-four hours of the day in half.

Pakok wasn't a town. It was a small SPLA outpost and was secluded, away from the local people of Anyuak. Because of its remoteness, we couldn't trade our clothing for corn with the Anyuak. The closest village called Aweyia was about a five hour's walk away. Only the SPLA soldiers went there because they had guns. The returnees travelled in large groups. Individuals who went to Aweyia often were robbed and killed. Even going there in a large group was risky since nobody had a gun. Because of that insecurity, we were confined to the Pakok area.

We stayed in Pakok for almost three months without a food supply. At that point, some hungry people devised a crazy idea of going back to Dimma to get food. When the SPLA had warned to evacuate the refugee camps early in June, some people didn't heed their evacuation order and had decided to stay.

After Mengistu's Ethiopian government collapsed, the SPLA sent some of its forces—led by two commanders, Bol Madut and Peter Parnyank—into Ethiopian territory to protect the refugees who were still in camps from Ethiopian forces. The new Ethiopian government viewed the presence of the SPLA forces in and around refugee camps as a violation of their sovereignty and wanted them out of their territory immediately. When those who had left Pakok to get food arrived back in Dimma, it was August and the Ethiopian government was tired of the refugees being there and violently forced them out.

Ethiopian forces attacked and captured the SPLA outpost in Coy River, several hours away from the Dimma camp, and then advanced toward it. Disaster soon befell the refugees. Fighting intensified between the SPLA and Ethiopian forces. Many of the returnees—including my friend, Joseph Deng, who had left Pakok to get food rations in Dimma—and those refugees who had refused to evacuate the camp in early June fled toward Jebel Rhad on the Sudan-Ethiopian border. Because the SPLA soldiers were mixed with the refugees, the Ethiopian soldiers indiscriminately fired on everyone. Many people died.

It was mid-August and the rainy season. There was a great deal of torrential rainfall, so the Rhad River overflowed. I was back in Sudan by then, but according to an account by Joseph Deng, one of the survivors of that ordeal, the current was so strong it washed away everything in its path. The flood waters uprooted trees along the riverbanks, carrying along huge downed trees at an incredible speed. At the river, people fleeing for their lives stopped. They were bewildered and confused, not knowing exactly how to cross the formidable and wildly flooding river.

Many people anxiously walked back and forth along the river. Others huddled in groups like buffalo or wild beasts, which also hesitate when they are afraid of crossing a river infested with crocodiles. Eventually, some people mustered up their courage and managed to swim across. Before everyone could, the Ethiopian forces caught up with the refugees and opened fired at those who were still on the wrong side.

With the Ethiopian soldiers shooting at them, people panicked and many desperately plunged into the river in an attempt to cross. Most of the refugees, including women and children, couldn't swim. Like ants, they climbed onto the backs of whoever they saw swimming, causing them to also drown. Huge logs swirling along in the flooded river smashed people's heads, knocking them unconscious and leaving them vulnerable to the ferocious current. Many were shot and others drowned. It was a chaotic and horrible scene. Those who survived the river crossing went to Jebel Rhad, the SPLA outpost, and then walked for three hours to Pakok and joined those who had been there since June.

Arrival in Pakok didn't mean all the challenges vanished into thin air. We were still dealing with a severe food shortage. The situation worsened once the number of returnees had doubled. We lived there for nine months without much food relief, from June 1991 through to January 1992. Later on, in August, we were told to build an airstrip in anticipation of relief agencies delivering food by air, but, unfortunately, they never did. In January 1992, food relief trucks finally made it to Pakok for the first time, but still the food rations were inadequate.

Here is what happened. When Mengistu's government began collapsing and the Ethiopian rebels advanced, the international relief agencies were hurridly trying to figure out where to move the Sudanese refugees. They decided we had to be relocated back in South Sudan; that way we wouldn't have to run later on when the Ethiopian government finally collapsed. That intention wasn't fulfilled because Sudan's military dictator, Bashir, banned relief agencies from operating along the Sobat

River. They had to get permission from the government before they could do anything. It was a runaround. The Sudanese government didn't want refugees to return. Based on my own interpretation, they probably thought if they allowed refugees to stay, the food delivered to those people, in those areas, would also be delivered to the SPLA.[12]

Even if the relief agencies had been allowed to supply food rations to returnees in Pakok and Pochalla, I believe their efforts by land would have been hampered by floodwaters because the road from Kapoeta to those two areas is inaccessible during the rainy season. Returnees in Pakok were not the only ones who experienced severe food shortages.

The returnees from Panyudo camp, who had crossed the Gilo River to the SPLA-held town of Pochalla, went through a similar ordeal from the day they left their camp. According to what I heard from my colleagues, James Manyiel Mayen and Chobany, who were there, they too experienced a severe food shortage. The Pochalla population was over 50,000. Pakok had an estimated 20,000 returnees. Pochalla's food situation became so dire they resorted to eating Waak, a certain tree that birds eat.

According to my friend, Manyiel Mayen, only small planes from the Red Cross made it to Pochalla early on when people arrived there. Those planes delivered a limited food supply, which the leaders distributed for consumption to 25,000 children and young people. In addition to one bag of flour, the minors received one sack of beans and a cow per 1,000 people every month. These cattle were collected by the SPLA from the Murle tribe in the Pibor area.

Unlike Pakok, where I was, the returnees in Pochalla were able to trade their belongings with the Anuak in nearby villages. The Anuak had

---

12   Johnson, *The Root Causes of Sudan's Civil Wars*, 89.

a good harvest of maize, so most people traded their clothing and shoes for food. In fact, anything that the Anuak liked and valued was sold to them for additional food.

Returnees in Pochalla spent almost three months without food relief. It reached them in August 1991 and lasted until January 1992. C-130 Hercules transport planes delivered food by air, dropping it off without even landing. Ultimately, the situation in Pakok was worse than in Pochalla. We never received any relief and were too far away from local villages to safely trade. If we went there without guns, they robbed us.

Chapter 13

Life as a Returnee in South Sudan

We lived in Pakok for nine months, from June 1991 to February 1992. Soon we were moving again.

Returnees from Dimma who stayed in Pakok walked to Boma, a journey over rugged terrain. After leaving Boma, it changed to plains with a few scattered trees. We reached Koragrab, then headed toward Kathangor Hills, and ventured into a semiarid plain. The only vegetation was short, thorny shrubs that buzzed when the wind blew on them. That region was still hot and humid. It was mid-February, the dry season, so there was no water. It took ten hours of walking to cross the Kathangor plain. After everybody converged in Magoth, we went to the town of Kapoeta. Then we moved to Narus near Kenyan border. The transportation to Narus was done by zones in Kapoeta until everyone had gone to Narus. That process took several weeks.

There were two main reasons we were moved to Narus. The first had to do with the hostile Toposa militia. Remaining in Kapoeta was not safe. The Toposa were unfriendly to the SPLA.

The Toposa people had been neglected and severely marginalized by Sudan's government. The government had never attempted to build schools. Because of a lack of government interest in educating their children, or providing any real support of any kind, the Toposa tribe was still backward and primitive. The men went naked, and the women wore hides, either cow or goatskin. They lived in thatch huts, but they had AK-47 rifles.

Even though Sudan's government did little to improve the lives of the Topoosa, they did engage in effective lies and propaganda. When the civil war started in 1983, the government turned to the Toposa and used them as a tool against the SPLA. The government warned them that the SPLA was comprised of the Dinkas, whose main goal was to dominate the Toposa people and steal their possessions. They told them the SPLA would take their livestock and abuse their girls. Sudan's government used that propaganda to put the Toposa against the SPLA and to undermine SPLA effectiveness in Eastern Equatoria. They armed the Toposa to fight the SPLA. Even after the SPLA had captured Kapoeta from the government, the Toposa traveled on foot to Juba, which is more than a 100 miles away, to get weapons from the government. Whenever SPLA soldiers or civilians left Kapoeta, for instance to pick firewood, the Toposa attacked and gunned them down. The threat of the Toposa confined us to town.

Another reason we were moved to Narus was the threat of continuing air raids by the government of Sudan, which indiscriminately attacked the SPLA and civilians as part of a new military offensive against us. The fall of Mengistu's regime in Ethiopia led to the SPLA losing its supply line. As a result, the Sudan dictator, Omar Al Bashir, saw an opportunity to wipe out the SPLA by launching what he called a "Big Offensive" in the dry season of 1992 to recapture all the towns held by the SPLA.

I believe what helped the government effort to recapture towns held by the SPLA was a widening split within the Sudanese rebel movement itself. The fall of the Ethiopian government would not have weakened the SPLA so much if it had remained cohesively as a unit. What was going on within the SPLA was like a civil war within a larger one. The

SPLA mainstream, the Torit faction, led by the SPLA founder, Dr. John Garang, fought on two fronts—the government, which was the main objective of rebellion, and a breakaway faction, the Nasir faction, led by Dr. Riek Machar.

Even though we weren't being bombed in Narus, we heard the rumbling sound of bombing and air raids in Kapoeta. Given the proximity to Narus, we always received the news about the air raids. In a SPLA town like Kapoeta, civilians and soldiers had to always be ready to run into trenches whenever there was one.

In the towns held by the SPLA, civilians and soldiers alike lived in constant fear of government air raids. Usually once, but sometimes twice, a week, government jets and Antonovs, a Russian-made turbo-prop transport plane, indiscriminately dropped bombs in towns, regardless of the presence of civilians. The government warplanes came from Juba, the capital of South Sudan, or Khartoum.

In April, we arrived in Narus, which was not really a town but an SPLA outpost. It was situated in a flat plain with vegetation of only short, thorny shrubs. The UNHCR made Narus an appropriate place for returnees after they had dug water pumps and brought plenty of food supplies.

We weren't provided with tents but with small plastic sheets. We made our own thatched huts because they weren't big enough to make tents. They were meant to protect individuals from rain when the rainy season approached in May. If it rained and two or three individuals joined their plastic sheets together, then they were able to protect themselves from the rain.

In Narus, we didn't have anything to do, except sit and eat. Every day I woke up and there was nothing to do; it was a very dull life. We did not even play soccer. The relief agencies did bring huge tents that they erected as storage for food. They had to provide something to keep it from spoiling because the rainy season was approaching. We didn't stay long in Narus; we had to leave in May.

On May 28, 1992, in a surprise attack, the government of Sudan, with the help of the Toposa militia, recaptured Kapoeta from the SPLA. When Ethiopian leader, Mengistu, was overthrown it had interrupted the SPLA supply, and that was when Kapoeta was captured.

At noon, the enemy shelled Kapoeta, and at one p.m. they attacked and captured it, displacing the civilians and a small number of SPLA soldiers who remained there. By that time, it was too late for additional SLA troops to get back to Kapoeta to defend it. SPLA commanders changed their strategy from offensive to defensive. They set up a base an hour away from Kapoeta, along the road leading to Kenya, to prevent government soldiers who had just retaken Kapoeta from tracking down the fleeing civilians.

Despite that protective effort by the SPLA, the Toposa militia killed many civilians as they fled to Narus, which is fifty-four miles, eighty-six kilometers, away from the Kenyan border. The terrain in the Kapoeta region is rugged topography with hills and ridges cut by shallow plains and seasonal streams. It is arid with very little vegetation, only thorny shrubs. The Toposa people, having lived there for centuries, have adapted to their hostile environment. They can run through this type of vegetation with ease. Besides, their movement was facilitated by the fact that they do not wear any clothing. When civilians fled, they could not move fast enough through that cat-claw thorny shrub. As a result, they had to stay on the main road leading to Narus where they fell vulnerable to constant attack by Toposa militias.

In the evening, the fleeing civilians reached Narus, where we stayed. By eight p.m. the whole camp was packed, and we flocked to the Kenyan border town of Lokichokio fifty-four miles away. I was scared and confused, and so was everybody else, about what was going to become of us. What intensified our fear was the fact that Narus is situated on the main road leading to Kapoeta and Kenya. The government forces could reach Narus in a matter of one hour.

We knew that there was fighting in Kapoeta, but we did not know whether the government forces had taken it or if it was still under the control of the SPLA until the fleeing civilians arrived. However, our leaders were informed about the whole situation, and were instructed to move everybody to Kenya when it got dark. We left at eight p.m. as part of our leaders' strategy to avoid an attack from the Toposa militia along the road to the Kenyan border. It was a smart move from our leaders. They saved our lives.

We walked through the night, carrying our food, bedding, and plastic sheets. The first group arrived in Lokichokio in the morning. Other people lagged behind and almost died of thirst and had to be rescued. The UNHCR used tankers to supply them with water along the way.

Walking, at first, was orderly when we left Narus. When we became tired, some people slowed down, and those who still had energy kept going. There were no organized groups; just a jumbled, exhausted stream of people. I arrived in the morning with the first group with my friend, Mayen. It took several hours for everyone to get to Lokichokio, and a week to figure out who had made it and who had not. When we arrived, we found that Lokichokio was in a desert-like region.

Upon arriving in Lokichokio, the Kenyan government and the UNHCR designated a flat area adjacent to the border where we were going to stay. No one was living there, and water was a big problem. The UNHCR brought water in tankers that they distributed for drinking and cooking. We waited in queues to get water. If your ration was not enough, no one gave you his or hers. You had to go back in the line for more. The first priority was given to drinking and cooking, but later on the UNHCR brought many tankers and so the issue of scarcity of water improved somewhat.

The living conditions in Lokichokio, Loki, were much worse than Narus. When we came to Loki, it was temporary; nothing was set up. The relief agency managing the temporary camp did not provide us with flour. They provided us with sorghum, wheat, lentils, beans, salt, and cooking oil. Some people tried to boil the grain and eat it by itself, but that caused stomach upset. Others tried to grind the grain on grinding rocks, but that caused even more severe diarrhea. During the grinding process, tiny grains of sand got into the flour. Many people became sick as a result.

The relief agency did not provide us with tents upon our arrival in Loki. We had to make do with the plastic sheets we had brought with us from Narus. When we arrived in Loki, the whole camp was poorly organized, except for minors, who had been organized into groups since Narus. Later on, when the camp leaders learned that we were going to be moved to a permanent camp, Kakuma, they came up with the idea of registering people in groups based on their regions, towns, and clans. Because of the camp's proximity to Sudan's border, the UNHCR was very concerned about the possibility that the Sudanese government might send its militia to attack refugees in the camp, or attack us with airstrikes. They came up with the idea of moving the refugees farther into Kenya to Kakuma. They brought trucks, lorries. Each group was called and transported to Kakuma right away.

The idea of organizing people in the communities into groups was proposed by our leader, Ajang Alaak. He believed that by staying in them, people would maintain their culture and bring up kids in a good way. In addition, people would be able to control criminality if they lived closer. Since we did not have any police to keep order, it was the best way for the people within the communities to watch out for one another and be able to watch out for and guard against the bad people among us.

Nobody really believed we were going to a different camp, except our leaders. We couldn't fathom why we were being moved. We were afraid the Kenyan government was going to hand us over to the Sudanese government. That rumor was prevalent among us. To reassure us, all the leaders—Deng Dau, Chol Deng Mareng, and Ajang Alaak—transported their groups first, starting with groups six and seven, comprised of people of Aweil, Northern Bahr el Ghazal State, and groups eight and twelve, comprised of people from Kongor in Jonglei state.

In the minors' groups, they transported group four, then group one and placed them next to group four. Group fifteen, to which I belonged, was brought after those groups. In Group fifteen, I lived with Lual Jala, Mathiang Marial, Joseph Makur, Mateny Mayen, and Abel Makoi. We stayed in Loki for almost two months before the UNHCR transported us to the new camp. They used trucks that brought food rations to transport us to Kakuma.

Chapter 14

My Cousin Offers Me a Great Opportunity

When we arrived in Kakuma, we found it to be a very inhospitable place. We were dropped off in a dusty, flat, semi-arid region located in the Turkana district in the Rift Valley. The place looked as flat as a parking lot. It was desolate; no one had been living there. Every now and then, a dust storm blew up and swept swiftly across the camp, making everything in its path look reddish. Prior to our arrival, the UNHCR had dug water pumps and planned the areas where each group was going to stay. We set up our tents right away, but they were temporary. Later on, we built our own thatched houses.

Initially, the food ration was insufficient. The NGO, non-government organization, that managed our food provided a certain type of sorghum grain that was not good for consumption. It was red and too difficult to pound, and did not produce enough flour. When we cooked it, it just looked like blood and was tasteless. Really, that type of grain is not suitable for human consumption, though maybe for horses and donkeys. That was the only food NGO brought.

When we became fed up with the NGO's way of managing the camp, our leaders negotiated for UNHCR to replace them as the camp manager. Because of our complaint, UNHCR handed over the management of Kakuma to Lutheran World Food Federation, LWF. LWF started out by providing us with rice and eventually brought us a variety of food items such as flour, beans, cooking oil, salt, lentils, and so forth. After LWF took over things improved.

We started school two weeks after our arrival in Kakuma. We attended a makeshift one under the trees, just as we had in the Dimma refugee camp when it was first established in 1986. Our teachers were other refugees, but later in 1993, after the schools were built, the UNHCR hired additional Kenyan teachers. The LWF brought school materials, but one of the most notable among them were portable blackboards. These standing blackboards suited the kind of school we had because they were easily folded and put away after classes were over. We were taught under the trees from 1992 to 1993 until the UNHCR built schools.

The construction of schools created employment for the refugees. The UNHCR gave contracts to refugees who had knowledge of that type of work. These contractors in turn hired refugees to build the school. My friends, Manyiel Mayen and Lual Jala, and my roommates, Makur Barnaba, Mathiang Marial, Mateny Mayen, and me worked for a contractor named Nyangkot Dut.

On December 24, 1993, my cousin, Deng—his dad and my father are brothers—who was in Nairobi, came to Kakuma to visit and celebrate Christmas. He was directed to the Dinka section and then found our clan, the Dinka Agar group. Deng was in the Ifo, currently called Dadab, refugee camp in the Garissa region in northeastern Kenya. When the dictator Mengistu was deposed in Ethiopia in May 1991, some Sudanese refugees fled in that direction.

Deng had completed his resettlement for the United States, and he visited Kakuma before his flight to America. He stayed through Christmas and the New Year, which was a festive time for us, even in Kakuma.

On Christmas Eve, we went to church in the evening, and people prayed until midnight. Then we went home to sleep; others stayed up and celebrated all night. We woke up around seven a.m., went to church around ten a.m., and danced, sang, and played drums. We cooked food and talked until the evening. Afterward, everyone went to parties, socialized, and had fun. Everybody had spent time praying and had honored God. Now it was time to get out and enjoy that for which what we were thankful. At the parties, each tribe had their own dances. It was very interesting. There were many varieties, and the different ones often went on simultaneously.

In Kakuma, I didn't miss home as much. We lived in communities and clans so everyone felt at home socializing with people with whom they could relate.

For us, New Year's Eve is about being with close friends and family. We partied and danced in thanks for everything that had passed the year before, reflecting on things we had done or should have done and looking forward to a new year and a new start. After the celebrations subsided, Deng went back to Nairobi to fly to the United States. Before he left, though, he and I had a cousin-to-cousin meeting.

He told me, "Ater, I am so excited to be so fortunate to have been admitted for resettlement to the US. What is your decision? Do you want to live here in Kakuma or would you like me to send you an affidavit of relationship when I get to America?"

An affidavit of relationship is a US immigration document that allows refugees in the United States to sponsor family members who also want to come to the US.

I replied, "I would rather go to America, because going there would provide me with many opportunities for a good education."

"Okay, great," Deng said. "I will send you an affidavit form, but you will have to travel to Ifo camp in northeastern Kenya where I pursued my resettlement process, because currently, there is no resettlement for Kakuma refugees yet."

After the meeting, we saw him off. His friends and I carried his luggage all the way to the bus, because in Sudanese culture a guest does not carry their own.

I hoped Deng would make it safely to the US and then I would be able to join him at some time in the future. After he departed, I resumed my ordinary life back in the camp. In April, I attended seventh grade class in Kakuma five days a week—Monday through Friday, from eight to two. Our teachers were a mixture of Sudanese and Kenyans. They taught us some English, but it was not much, just the basics. That was my life for many months in Kakuma.

In October 1994, Deng sent the affidavit of relationship form, addressed to the Ifo refugee camp (Dadaab) in northeastern Kenya to his friend in Nairobi, Khamis Masharanga. Deng also enclosed 200 US dollars for my transportation from Kakuma to Nairobi and then to Ifo. Once Khamis received the money, he talked to a friend of his, Solomon Monhdit, who was a driver, and asked him to get me at Kakuma and drive me to Nairobi. Monhdit picked me up in a small Geo Metro, and around three p.m. handed me a letter from Deng.

In it, I read that Deng had sent me $200. I had never before seen a dollar sign so I asked Monhdit what the symbol meant, but he did not know it either. At that point, the $200 mentioned in the letter did not make any sense to me. It turned out Khamis had kept the $200, not knowing that Deng had mentioned it in the letter. When I arrived in Nairobi, all Khamis handed me was the affidavit of relationship form along with a small bag of sugar and rice he had gotten for me. I asked him about the money, but he said that he had spent it on the sugar and rice that I could take with me to the camp. I did not care; I just asked for enough money for a bus to Ifo.

In Nairobi, I stayed with Khamis for about two weeks. He was living at the apartment of my cousin's uncle, Maker Benjamin. In 1994, my cousin, Deng, met Khamis there and they became friends. Therefore, Deng used him as a liaison to facilitate my transportation from Kakuma to Nairobi and all the way to my final destination, Ifo. Khamis knew Nairobi well because he had lived there for several years, and so I depended on him entirely.

Benjamin, with whom I stayed, was a very kind and hospitable man. Even though he had little money he allowed boys like us to stay at his apartment temporarily before they went back to either the Kakuma or Ifo camps. To me, his apartment was like a transit point. I needed to stay there for a while in order to make all the necessary arrangements for the Ifo refugee camp. I was very appreciative of Benjamin's kind help.

At Ifo, I'd be able to follow up on my process for resettlement to the US. Life in Nairobi was strikingly worse for me than Kakuma. Compared to Nairobi, life in Kakuma was pleasant and leisurely. I didn't need transportation to anywhere I wanted to go. I was able to just walk around, visiting friends and playing soccer.

However, in Nairobi, I had to stay indoors most of the time. Sometimes I went out and walked among the little markets, but for transportation anywhere else in the city, such as downtown, I needed money. Most people, including me, had very little as few people had jobs.

Sudanese refugees who had documents from the UNHCR in Nairobi contacted nongovernmental organizations in the city, and that way they would get some financial assistance. Despite the fact they had documents, it didn't guarantee automatic help. To them it was like fishing. One day you got lucky, and another you came home emptyhanded. That was how Sudanese refugees used to survive in Nairobi back then. However, since I had come from Kakuma, I didn't have any papers to qualify for cash assistance. I had no job.

At the Nairobi apartment there was rarely any food in the refrigerator. Those who were going out bought meals. Then when they came home, they'd bring food for me to eat. I wasn't starving, but I did not eat during the day and was often hungry.

People staying in the apartment left every morning, saying to me, "Ater, we're going out. See you later." That was it. They did not have jobs. They'd just go and look for some money from nongovernmental agencies. That's how they lived there. They had documents so they qualified for assistance from the NGOs. I did not see them again until late in the evening. Day in and day out, I was on the couch, waiting for them like an inmate in a prison cell.

It was a very dull life for a young person. Sometimes, I went out and walked around in the little markets.

The Kawangware market is on Kawangware Road. Local farmers brought all kinds of fruits and vegetables and displayed them alongside the road. There were a few stores and bars as well. After spending two weeks in an apartment that felt like a jail cell to me, I asked Khamis if I should make plans to go to Ifo, where the UNHCR would provide me with food rations so I wouldn't have to be hungry anymore.

Three Dinka guys, Agustino, Achuiel, and Forgew, had come to Nairobi from Ifo to get some pocket money. When they returned to Ifo refugee camp, I went with them. We set out in the morning, first to the bus station in downtown Nairobi where we would take a bus through Garissa, Dadaab, and finally to Ifo. That was where I could pursue my resettlement to the United States.

At the bus station, we found four buses heading to Garissa, all full with Somali nationals. Apparently, that was because Garissa is in the northeastern part of Kenya and mostly populated with Somalis.

Culturally and traditionally, the people of the Garissa region are still connected to Somalia.

The buses were packed, hot, and sticky. There was no air conditioning. It was my first time being around so many Muslims, and few of them could speak either English and or Dinka. I was so thankful to have those guys from Ifo with me for the ten hours the trip took because we were able to converse in our native language.

The bus did not stick to any sort of schedule I was able to discern. There were no stops; it stopped whenever the driver saw passengers standing on the roadsides. Villagers went to the roadside and waited patiently for a bus.

The drivers made no effort whatsoever to manage the number of people on the bus. We were packed like chickens in a cage, so close to other people that I breathed air onto the neck of the person in front of me. The smells of others so close was unpleasant—their bad breath, body odor, food, and dirty clothing. At times, groups of passengers disembarked, and I enjoyed some respite, able to briefly stand in the middle aisle, stretch my legs and enjoy some fresh air. Then more people got onto the bus, and we were packed together again.

Chapter 15

Threat of Shifters, Bandits, on the Road

Occasionally, the buses stopped at small stations so the passengers were able to get some rest and food. During those stops, we bought milk, tea, and chapattis, which are thin pan-fried bread. Chapattis taste like croissants but are flat like tortillas. They make a good snack, and at the same time, are filling. They have the added benefit of being cheap. Some people also bought roasted corncobs. Vendors set up their grills beside the roads and roasted fresh corncobs from the farm. They mixed salt and pepper in a bowl, and then cut limes and kept them in a separate bowl. Once a customer made a purchase, they gave them a cut lime so they could dip it into salt and pepper and smear it onto the corncob. For those who didn't like pepper, they only used the lime and salt. Eventually, we all packed back onto the bus.

By the time we came close to Garissa, the bus was greeted by policemen who were escorting buses because of shifters—highwaymen who robbed people on the roads, including buses and cars. They are called shifters because they'd shift their locations every now and then. Since the Garissa region is so close to the border of Somalia, most of the shifters come from there. They dress like ordinary people, so there is no way you can tell who is a shifter and who is not.

The shifters hung out in towns and spied on people, both Somalis and foreigners alike. After they pinpointed their target, they went and laid in wait in ambush. They robbed people of money, clothing, and even cars. They'd take anything of value from their victims. Sometimes they killed people. If they stopped and robbed people in a car, they'd steal it and drive it to Somalia and vice versa; they also stole cars in Somalia and brought them to the Garissa region. It was a very hostile environment for travelers. The only people relatively safe from shifters were the very poor, who had nothing of worth to steal.

We arrived in Garissa at five p.m. We were exhausted, and I suggested we spend the night there at a lodge, but my three Sudanese friends insisted we leave the same night. I said to them, "Folks, let's spend the night and wait for the bus to Dadaab tomorrow." I didn't want to appear like a coward. All I wanted was for all of us to be safe. They didn't listen to me. They said we had to leave, so we went and rented a rickety Land Rover. It was gray-looking and full of dents. A worrisome *tut tut* sound occurred when the vehicle was running.

A Somali businessman drove the Land Rover to carry goods from Garissa to Dadaab. I told my friends, "I don't know the area that much. You have been to Ifo before so you should know how far it is from Garissa, but I suspect this car won't get us to Dadab because it isn't in good shape." I turned to the driver and asked him, "Are you sure your car will get us to Dadaab?"

He replied, "Yes, it will take us for sure."

We collected some money and paid the driver. At around seven p.m. we left Garissa. The Land Rover broke down halfway between Garissa and Dadaab. We saw Somali herdsmen with AK-47s on their backs, driving camels. I was scared. The driver assured us he could fix the car because his business partner was going to deliver some parts for him. He recommended we stay with him. It was too dangerous to go on foot to Dadaab due to the presence of shifters in the area. He wanted us to spend the night there with him and wait until the other car came. My friends were impatient. They said no, we should walk and cover the remaining distance on foot.

I asked my friends, "How are we going to walk while we don't even have any weapons with which to protect ourselves? You guys know shifters are around here."

My friends did not listen to my pleas, so we left the broken-down Land Rover and set off walking. I felt it was a very stupid, risky move. It was pitch black; there was no moonlight, and we did not have flashlights. Whenever we spotted a car coming toward us, we ran into the bushes. We never knew if they might shoot us, thinking we were shifters.

I told my buddies, "We need to come up with rules of the road."

They looked at me in a weird way, and said, "What rules of the road are you talking about?"

"Guys, if we encounter shifters, we should not run in different directions but as a group," I told them. "If we scatter, we won't be able to find one another in the dark and eventually they will kill us one by one when the morning dawns."

They didn't come up with any better plan, so I continued, "Okay, shifters have weapons, so what we need to do is to cut some branches and make them look like guns."

We did the best we could, fashioning sticks to look like guns, and I told them we needed some space between us while walking.

"Let's walk like we have guns," I told them. "I am going to lead the group, and if I see something suspicious, I will yell out, 'Lie down!'"

After we had walked for about four hours, we heard footsteps of several people approaching. As soon as they saw us, they ran in different directions, and we too ran back a few meters and lay down beside the road. We couldn't tell who they were and whether they carried guns because it was so dark. They might have been local people who thought we were shifters, or they might have feared we were from a rival clan.

After we made sure it was safe to continue, we got up from our hiding place and ran forward where they had left the road. We passed where we had encountered them and came to a lake and drank some water. We were so thirsty from walking nearly seven hours through the night with nothing to drink. It was a half an hour walk to Dadaab from where that incident took place. It occurred at about four in the morning. We arrived in Dadaab at around five a.m. because we rested for about half an hour after the shifters' ordeal. When we related our story to local people in Dadaab, they were stunned. They couldn't believe how we had made it through. From Dadaab, we walked to the Ifo refugee camp, which only took about twenty minutes.

In Ifo, there were Somali and Sudanese refugee camps. The Sudanese camp was very small relative to Kakuma. It was comprised of four groups—Dinka, Equatorians, which encompassed all the tribes from the Eastern and Western Equatoria region of Southern Sudan—Anyuak, and Nuer.

The Ifo refugee camp lay in the semi-arid zone. It got very hot and humid with little rainfall. Initially, when we Sudanese refugees arrived in the Ifo camp, the Somalis didn't like us. Wherever we went, kids would hold their noses and throw stones at us, and say, "Uf Christo." What they meant by "uf" is that we Christians stink because we use stuff like toilet paper when we use the bathroom and they use water. "Uf" in Somali means stink.

We were the minority in the camp and whole town. There were Islamic Madrasas schools, where they taught little children the Koran. They carved verses from it into wood. Each kid memorized them. You'd hear them in the morning, as they memorized the lines.

All the businesses were controlled by the Somalis. I felt as if I lived in Somalia. Wherever I went, I kept hearing the words "Uf Christo." I hated it and so did other Sudanese refugees. What could we do in response? We couldn't fight the whole town. If we tried, they would wipe us out. We sucked it up and just lived with it. We got used to it. Sometimes, we played soccer against the Somali team. If we won, they attacked us and threw stones at us. When they won, we did nothing to them. Eventually, they became more accepting of us and became a bit tolerant.

On March 25, 1995, after I had spent five months in Ifo, officials with the Joint Voluntary Agency, JVA, flew from Nairobi to Ifo in a small plane and then handed out forms to refugees for resettlement. The JVA works with the US Immigration and Naturalization Service, INS, whose job it is to screen refugees for admission to the United State. I didn't yet have strong skills speaking or writing English, so I filled out the form with the help of my friend, Lual Jala. I turned it in, hoping that was a first step in my journey to the United States. Little did I understand then how well-versed I eventually would become in the complex processes a refuguee faces when seeking resettlement to the US.

My cousin, Deng, who was then living in North Dakota, had begun his process for his resettlement to the US at the Ifo refugee camp in 1994. Deng filed the affidavit of relationship form, as a sponsor to me, with the Lutheran Social Services. Deng sent the original to the INS office in the US embassy in Nairobi, and sent me a copy. The affidavit claimed I was Deng's cousin and that he'd sponsor me when I got to the United States.

On April 1, 1995, the JVA came back and interviewed us. Two weeks later, our names were posted on the board in front of the UNHCR, United Nations refugee agency, compound. Every year the US admits a certain number of refugees for resettlement. According to UNHCR policies, refugees can cross into any neighboring country if their lives are in danger. From that country, where they have refugee status, they can't move to another country unless the UNHCR approves it. Therefore, any country that is willing to sponsor refugees has to go through the UNHCR. After it obtains UNHCR's approval, then the country can go ahead and apply whatever criteria they want to use to process refugees to come to their nations.

That was what the United States did. They had agreed to allow resettlement of about 3,000 Sudanese refugees who wanted to come to the US and live a better life. The US consulted with the UNHCR, and when they received a go-ahead, the JVA came to Ifo and started interviewing us.

The US immigration official who interviewed me was an attorney named Ronald. That was as close as I had ever been to a white man. His eyes were blue like cat's eyes. My friend, Jala, stood beside me to translate. Ronald first asked me what would happen to me if I were to go back to Sudan. He questioned me on what I had put down on my form. Ronald asked what had caused me to leave my hometown. I described why I felt they should qualify me as a refugee. For example, he wanted to hear me say that if I returned to Sudan, the government might imprison or kill me.

The INS screens out people who do not qualify for resettlement. Some people would do anything to get to go to America, including making up stories about their background. There was one Ethiopian guy who spoke Arabic—I don't know whether he had ever lived in Sudan— and he tried to lie about being Sudanese. He eventually failed because the INS goes into great detail exploring personal histories with refugees.

During my interview with Ronald, I explained in Dinka how I had arrived at the refugee camp. Jala translated my narrative into English while Ronald peered intently into my eyes.

The night before, Jala had coached me on how to present myself during the interview.

"When you go in tomorrow morning, please make sure you look in the attorney's eyes as you explain your story to him," Jala had told me. "Most people fail just because they don't look at the interviewer's eyes. The attorneys think they're lying."

In our culture, it is considered very rude to look into a person's eyes, but to Americans like Ronald, direct eyecontact is considered a sign of candor. The advice from my friend made a big difference in my interview. Otherwise, I am certain I would have failed. We heard stories of Sudanese refugees who had strong cases to make for resettlement but who failed their interviews because they talked while looking at the floor.

So even though it made me uncomfortable, I talked while making eyecontact with Ronald. At first, I was very anxious, worried that I was failing the interview. I described my personal history and what I had been through while Ronald listened intently.

One way the INS weeded out refugees was to provide them with forms to fill out, which they took with them back to Nairobi. Later, they sent a letter to the UNHCR at the refugee camp with the names of the people they had decided to interview. When they came back for the second time it was specifically for interviewing. They had the forms in front of them, but the person being interviewed didn't have a copy. They looked carefully for discrepancies between the forms and the in-person interview.

Ronald used that same tactic with me. During my interview, every now and then he interrupted me to ask, "Well, you said this in your form, but now you're saying something different." Then I clarified my answers with him.

Two weeks after the interview, the names of those who had passed the interviews were posted again on a board in front of the UNHCR compound. As soon as word got out that the names had been posted, people ran to see whether their names were on the list.

It was around two p.m. when I heard that important news. It was very hot and humid that day. We were playing cards in the shade under the trees. I ran as fast as my legs could take me. My heart was still beating very fast. That was a defining moment for me. I was very nervous, because failing the interview meant more suffering and hardship to me. Where would I go? How would I live in this camp with no hope and no goal? The hope of coming to the US was what enabled me to withstand all the suffering and hardship I had gone through.

When I reached the board, I started to sweat profusely. I quickly looked over the board and scanned the list to the letter "M" because the names were listed alphabetically by last names. Bingo! There I saw my last name—Malath. I sighed, the sigh of great relief. I had successfully cleared one important hurdle; now I had to worry about the next step—medical screening.

Chapter 16

Back to Nairobi. Finding a Shack in the Kibera Slum

In May 1995, all of us who had passed their interview were told to go to Nairobi for medical screening. A medical checkup was necessary. We had to do it; otherwise, we wouldn't get to go to the US. The INS didn't want people who were HIV positive to come to the US. If you were found to have other diseases, which were curable, they allowed you a period for treatment and then, if you recovered, you were allowed to resettle. Not so if you were found to be HIV positive. That effectively shut the door to any chance of resettlement to the United States.

Unfortunately, neither the INS nor UNHCR provided us with money for transportation to Nairobi or accommodations for the duration of the medical checkup. We had to sell some of our food rations and then board a bus to Garrisa and from there to Nairobi. Once we arrived in Garrisa, we spent the night at a lodge.

Jala and I decided to celebrate our passing of the interview by eating Khat (street names Chat and Miraa), which is widely consumed in Kenya, just like coffee in the Western world. Khat looks greenish and tastes like spinach. In Dadaab, there was a small plane that delivered Khat every morning. Dadaab is fairly close to Ifo, and from Ifo we could see it hovering. As soon as the plane neared, before it landed, people flocked to the airstrip and in a flash formed a queue. Young and old alike waited in line to buy Khat, just like when people in the US form a line in the morning to get lattes at Starbucks. People chewed it, and police did not bother them about it at all. To them, it was like coffee is regarded in America. Nobody thought he or she were using drugs. Truck drivers chewed it to keep alert overnight.

Jala and I bought a kilo of green leaves and chewed it overnight. In the beginning when I started chewing it, I was able to maintain my saliva, but as I kept chewing and chewing, my mouth got drier and drier. Some people chewed it with a little bit of sugar to keep their mouths from getting dry. I personally believe Khat is a drug based on the effect I experienced after chewing it. It took about half an hour to feel it, and I became somewhat hyperactive and very emotional about everything I was going through in life. I felt sad and depressed. In the morning all the melancholy I had felt just vanished into thin air.

We boarded a bus for Nairobi. The INS and the UNHCR didn't coordinate how we were going to go about doing medical screening. The INS paid for medical bills, but they expected everybody knew somebody in Nairobi. Therefore, finding a place to stay in Nairobi over the course of screening and orientation was left up to us.

It was early May 1995 when Jala and I arrived in Nairobi from the Ifo refugee camp for medical screening. At first, we settled in with his uncle's widow, Akuac Mayom, who had moved to Nairobi from Kakuma refugee camp after her husband passed away so her kids could go to a better school. Next to her apartment, on the opposite side of the street, lived Fatna Kok and her husband, Magok Manyol. Both families belonged to our clan, Dinka Agar.

Jala and I initially stayed at Akuac's home. It was a three-bedroom apartment in a highrise estate with a small living room, sitting room, kitchen, and one bathroom. Seven people lived there before we came. We lived with this single mom with five children—three sons and a daughter and stepson—plus one adult male relative who came from Kakuma. I really appreciated her kindness in letting us stay at her apartment despite the fact it was already so overcrowded. We lived there for a couple of weeks. Over the course of our stay, we depended on her for accommodations and food. She really wanted to help us out, but her situation was even worse than our own. She was a single mom raising that many kids with no permanent income. She had relatives overseas who paid for her children's school fees.

"I am going to leave, but you should stay with your relatives," I suggested to Jala. "There is no reason whatsoever for you to be stressed out about where to stay while you have a place such as this one."

He replied, "Ater, I know the situation is tough for my uncle's family, but there is no way I will remain in this apartment. We will leave together. We have been through hardship together in Kakuma and Ifo camps and so there is nothing that is going to separate us." He added, "This is going to ruin my reputation if you are seen suffering while I am living comfortably with my relatives."

We didn't know where to go at that point. We were unemployed and had no connections. It seemed we were going to end up being homeless, roaming the streets of Nairobi. To be homeless there is difficult, especially if you're not a citizen. The many homeless in the streets might have killed us had we decided to become homeless. They likely would have perceived us as competitors.

Moreover, there were people in Nairobi who didn't like refugees, in part because a few well-educated Sudanese held good jobs with nongovernmental organizations. Many Kenyans in Nairobi made false stereotypical generalizations that all Sudanese refugees were rich. Occasionally, our people were robbed when they went out at night. Some Kenyan police officers, as well as thugs who impersonated police, extorted

Sudanese refugees. Usually, the police did not immediately imprison my people. Instead, they detained them for long periods of time, waiting until they could come up with some money.

At one point, I was detained for around two hours by the police. Over the course of my detention, I was somewhat scared, but at the same time it didn't bother me that much. I knew that even if they took me to jail, what were they going to get from me? I merely looked into their eyes calmly as they questioned me.

One of the police officers asked me, "Do you know anybody who could come and get you out of here? If you don't, we will take you to jail."

I replied, "No, I know nobody, and I think no one is going to come and get me out of here." I just stared at them, looking very calm.

Throughout my brief detention, I heard the police officers converse in Swahili every now and then. It made me uncomfortable. I didn't know the language that well, so whenever they talked like that I wondered, *What the hell is going to come out of this?* When people talk in a language that we don't understand, we automatically assume they are saying bad things about us. It is human nature.

I think so many law enforcement officers in Nairobi resorted to corruption because of a lack of better living wages. Some police officers even on their days off put on their uniforms and went into the streets at night to round us up and extort us for money.

They turned on Sudanese refugees for several reasons. First, refugees received some cash assistance—those who lived in Nairobi—from nongovernmental organizations such as UNICEF, the Red Cross, the IRC, or religious organizations. Therefore, they were seen as a source of extra income by some rogue police officers as well as thugs. Second, a number of refugees sold some of their food rations in Kakuma and then came to Nairobi to buy nicer clothing and other necessities, so the police wanted to get extra money from them before they had a chance to spend it. If they detained a person and he or she gave them money, no matter how little the amount, they usually let that person go and moved on, looking for someone else to extort.

In my case, I didn't have money, but they did not initially believe that, so they kept me there for a couple of hours. I continued to repeat the same stance, "I don't have any money, nor do I know anybody who does."

Finally, they asked me where I lived. When I answered I was living in the nearby Kibera Slum, they finally concluded they were not going to be able to wring any money out of me or anyone I knew. One of the officers said, "Let him go," in Swahili. I walked for about five minutes back to my little shack. They had concluded I was just a penniless Sudanese refugee, living in the Kibera Slum.

We had ended up in the Kibera Slum after concluding as bad as that option was, it was better than roaming the streets as homeless Sundanese. Jala made the decision during an emergency meeting to figure out what to do next. Jala said if we lived on the streets our situation would likely get worse and we'd never make it to the United States. Instead, he proposed we should find a place to live in the Kibera Slum. I immediately disagreed with him, very wary of Kibera's terrible reputation as incredibly dangerous with many gangs residing there. I had heard about and seen the result of horrible crimes committed in that place.

While we were still living at the highrise apartment, one night, criminals robbed a man, slit his throat, and then laid his body across the railroad tracks so it looked as if a train had run over and killed him. In the morning, when the police investigated the incident, they determined the victim was murdered by gangs.

It was a very dangerous environment. One night at about seven p.m., as Jala and I walked along the railroad to the highrise apartment, a group

Lual Jala and me at Highrise apartments

of thugs armed with machetes attacked us. Some came behind us and the rest ran up in front of us. Their goal was to force us to run toward a stone fence where we would have no way of getting out. Fortunately, we quickly discerned what they planned and outran them before they had a chance to cut us off.

Kibera Slum, Nairobi, Kenya 1995

I was 19 year old in Kibera slum in Nairobi, Kenya, 1995.

Kibera is the biggest slum in Africa and one of the largest in the world. It houses nearly one million people. The government owns all the land. About ten percent of its population is made up of shack owners, and many of them own many other shacks that they rent out. We went there and met with an old woman who appeared to be in her late fifties and owned two shacks. We contacted this woman and explained our situation—that we were trying to emigrate to America and that we needed a place to stay while we awaited medical screening.

As we told our story, the old woman's eyes opened wide with surprise and amazement, as if to imply, *You guys are Sudanese? What makes you come and live here while most of your people live in nicer apartments?* She thought most Sudanese were rich, and then she was doubly surprised to realize that not all are. After she paused for a few seconds, she said, "I am going to rent you one of my shacks for a hundred shillings a month." One hundred shillings was a little less than $1.50 back then. The exchange rate was seventy shillings for a dollar in the black market.

We were ecstatic to have found a place to live. We went back to Fatna Kok and informed her that we had found housing in Kibera and that we just needed some help with cooking utensils. She provided us with a stove, several dishes, and a mattress. We would put that mattress on the floor in our newly acquired shack.

The average shack in Kibera measures about twelve feet by twelve feet, built with screen or mud walls that are plastered with concrete. Most have a tin roof and a dirt or concrete floor. Some shacks house up to eight or more people, many sleeping on the floor. There is no privacy in the Kibera Slum because of the close proximity of each dwelling.

In our shack, which was next to our property owner, we heard almost everything occurring in our surrounding neighbors' shacks. If somebody made love to his girlfriend or wife, we heard that too. Our landlady was a very pious and religious person. Every morning, she listened to gospel music, and we listened to it as well.

About eighty percent of Kibera has no electricity or clean water. Most of Kibera doesn't have running water or toilet facilities. Nearly fifty shack dwellers typically share one latrine, a hole in the ground. During the day, some people defecated into plastic bags and threw them into nearby ditches at night. They called this process of throwing feces at night a flying toilet. It's incredibly filthy and unsanitary. Those who had a latrine

113

and water charged people money for using them despite the fact that people couldn't even afford food. Luckily, we didn't go through that. We went to the highrise to use either Fatna's or Akuace's toilet. We eventually bathed there as well.

Since there were no Dumpsters, trash lay everywhere, creating foul and extremely unhealthy living conditions. Disease is prevalent. One problem we had to deal with occurred because of the way some shacks were built on higher ground than others, specifically our own. A ditch was usually dug from those places down the hill, and during rainstorms, all kinds of filth-laden water ended up at our doorstep.

Our landlady often said, "Do you guys believe in God? You need to pray. Keep praying, one day you will succeed."

To this we dutifully replied, "Yes, we do pray."

Every morning Jala and I went out to ask some Sudanese for money. Sometimes we got as much as twenty shillings. If we did get some money, we didn't take a bus home; we walked and saved it for food. On our way, we stopped at the open market next to Kibera where fruit and vegetables were sold. Generally, we bought two tomatoes, Royco, a type of seasoning, two bundles of kale, and a packet of ugali, ground corn flour. Then we went home, lit our stove, and prepared our dinner.

Chapter 17

Medical Screening and Fear of HIV

Later that month, we were called in for medical screening. We were very anxious about the test—at that time most of my people didn't know much about HIV or AIDS. I recalled a guy named Dut who tested positive for HIV. Whenever he came out to where Sudanese people partied and had fun, they avoided contact with him. Most falsely believed AIDS was contagious like tuberculosis. At parties, Dut was served food and drink and then was left alone. Dut was a social outcast. Jala and I were terrified that we'd be shunned like Dut if we tested HIV positive, and that it would bar us from going to the United States.

We were incredibly anxious about the test. "Ater, if I test HIV positive, I will walk and walk all the way toward South Africa in order to die there," Jala said to me.

I commiserated with my friend. "If I am tested positive, I will run underneath a matatu (a minivan) and die instantly."

We often engaged in that type of worried conversation late at night after we ate dinner and before bed.

On June 16, 1995, we were called for a medical screening. The INS paid for everything. All we had to do was to show up on our scheduled date. We went to the hospital very early in the morning, around eight o'clock. It was in the middle of downtown Nairobi.

In the hospital, on the day of our appointment, Jala and I heard a lady screaming as she came down the elevator. I asked, "What the hell is going on in the elevator?" I thought someone was beating up a woman in there.

Then one guy said, "Oh, her husband failed the HIV test. That's why she is crying. Since he is the head of the household, the whole family is no longer going to the US."

A few people failed the HIV test. I was especially worried, because at some point in time I had practiced unprotected sex. The thought of being HIV positive bothered me tremendously as I sat and prepared to have my blood drawn.

Jala and I walked into the room like rain-soaked chickens attempting to become dry. We were so scared we twitched and constantly shifted our eyes. The nurse came and called me by my last name, "Mr. Malath, have a seat." She drew my blood and then told me that I should come back for the result in two weeks. She did the same procedure for my friend, Jala.

Our worries were intensified by the fact that everybody in the community was curious about the results of our test. Wherever we went, people asked, "When are your results going to come out?" Every day Jala and I prayed in order for God to turn things around for us. We couldn't handle being both virtually homeless and HIV positive.

Two weeks later, we went back to the hospital to receive our results. Suddenly, the doctor came out of his office and called my name. My heart beat very fast. He said, "Mr. Malath, be seated." I was incredibly nervous. This was a defining moment in my life. At that point, Jala and I were astonishingly malnourished because of insufficient food in the slum and the high level of stress we were going through. When we looked at ourselves, it was as if we had AIDS. Indeed, some people thought we had the disease. As I sat there sweating, the doctor pulled out my file, and said, "Mr. Malath, you have no syphilis, you have no tuberculosis, and you're also HIV negative." I immediately jumped to my feet with excitement, went out, and told Jala that my test came out negative.

Instantly, Jala's shoulders dropped and his facial expression shrunk after I told him that I had tested negative. I didn't know what was going on in his mind, but upon later reflection, I understood he was probably thinking about what would become of him if he turned out positive. He would be alone. I was also concerned. I did not want to split up with my best friend. Jala went into the room, and about five minutes later, and came out with a big smile. He hugged me and then said: "Ater, we made it!"

Even though we were from a different country, people in the Kibera Slum accepted us as their own. Sometimes, neighbors would invite us to the nearby bar and buy us cheap locally brewed beer. Often they asked us why we chose to live in the slum. We answered that we were poor and that our people didn't like us.

The only person we told the true reason of our stay in Kibera was the landlady. One guy said to us, "Don't worry about what people say about Kibera. We were born here and will get old and die here. Don't pay attention to what they say about life here." In fact, inhabitants of Kibera did not feel as if they were living in a bad place at all; they have accepted it.

Three months later, in mid-September, the IOM, International Organization for Migration, gave out money to refugees who had passed their medical check-ups. The IOM is like a liaison between the INS and the UNHCR. The IOM receives funding from the US government to facilitate the transportation of refugees who have been accepted to emmigrate to the United States.

I don't know whether someone informed the IOM that some people were suffering or they decided on their own to provide assistance. For some reason, after we finished the medical screening and were going through orientation, the IOM provided 2,000 shillings per person. I received that money for September only and then flew to the US on September 24, 1995. I wish they had done that early on.

The IOM had rented a facility toward Kangware estate. It had a brick fence and two brick buildings. All those who passed the medical screening went there for orientation. I remember our instructor was from Somalia. He had emmigrated to the United States during the 1980s and stayed for almost ten years; he returned to Africa. He told our class, "If you go to America, make sure you go to school and educate yourself, because if you don't you will end up doing an unskilled job like me." He told us that because he didn't go to college he ended up being a dishwasher in America.

The instructor showed us a video about gangs in America and advised us not to associate with them. He explained to us many things about our new country.

"Don't ever ask somebody how much he or she makes," the instructor told us. "Don't loan money to people you don't know or even friends. And finally, don't get involved in prostitution because it is illegal in the United States."

While living in the Kibera Slum the idea of going to America often seemed impossible, out of reach. At times, I almost gave up on the idea, but after I thought of the hardships I had gone through, I ruled out that idea completely. My life for years had been enduring one hardship after another, constantly wandering around hungry. What really encouraged me was the fact that my medical screening was negative.

Most people in my community didn't know what was going to become of us after we got to the US. The fear of the unknown was so prevalent, giving rise to wild rumors, such as that people who traveled to America were not allowed to return to Africa. Many were skeptical of why the United States allowed people to go there for better lives. Some became so frightened they gave up efforts to emigrate to the US.

A woman named Ayen, from our clan, was suspicious of why we were going to America. She said to me, "Ater, I think you are not going to come back to Africa."

I assured her that I was willing to take the risk for hope of a better life.

"Nowadays, America is different from what it was in the past," I told her. "Now, it's a modern time. I don't think Americans enslave people anymore."

Chapter 18

News from Home

I did not hear of my parents' whereabouts for ten years, until 1995 when I was nineteen. I had last seen them when I was nine years old, before our village was attacked and I fled with my Uncle Mangar. While I lived in the Kibera Slum with my friend, Lual Jalal, I encountered another one of my uncles, Mabor, who happened to be working for NGOs, delivering food rations to various areas in Southern Sudan, including the town of Akot. That was close to the village where my mother lived with my younger siblings, who were born while I was in the refugee camp in Ethiopia. My uncle informed me that my dad had passed away from heart disease. He suggested I should have some photos taken of me that he could deliver to my mother and siblings whenever he went back there again.

I was reluctant to give him my pictures because I was so malnourished. I did not want my younger siblings, who had never seen me, to form a first impression of me in that state. I was not worried about my mom seeing me looking so frail.

Me while living in Kibera slum before my flight to the USA

She is my mother. She knew how I used to look before I reached that stage.

"Ater, don't care about how you look," Jala said to me. "Your siblings were born after you were gone, man. This is very important. They will know the hardship you are currently in and why you are so skinny. So, the main thing right now is not about your appearance but to send those pictures so they know you are alive. They want proof of that. I think that is why Uncle Mabor insists on taking your pictures home."

Jala was successful in convincing me. The next day, he and I went to downtown Nairobi, and I had my photos taken. I gave them to Mabor and kept one for myself.

Before I had heard about the death of my dad, while I was still in the Katama refugee camp, I had a feeling that something had happened to him. He would come to me in a dream every night right after I fell asleep. I could vividly recognize his appearance. After I went to bed and before I fell deeply asleep, my dad would slap me like when somebody is trying to wake me up. I would startle and wake up as a result. When I was fully awake, I would realize it was a dream, not actually my dad who had physically slapped me. Jala would hold me down. After he woke me up, then I would go back to sleep. It continued for a very long time. He kept coming to me in a dream in that manner.

Jala and I shared a bed and, as a result, he often had to deal with holding me down when those dreams happened. If there are not enough beds, it is a customary thing for guys or girls to share one bed. Jala and I alternated—because guys have broader shoulders—one of us faced his head in one direction and the other did likewise so we could fit in the bed.

As soon as I heard from Mabor that my dad had passed away, I questioned him right away about what had happened. Mabor said that he did not know what kind of heart disease my father had had. Medical care was poor in the isolated village where my father had lived. Travel was dangerous. As a result, he could not get medicine. Another town, Wau, where people could get it was about 136 miles away from where my parents were living at the time when his health deteriorated.

Though saddened by the news of the death of my dad, I appreciated the information from home on my parents and siblings brought to me by Mabor. Our meeting was happenstance; he did not know I was living in Kibera. He had come to visit one of his friends named Mayom Athian, who lived in Uwungumu estate in Nairobi. Mabor heard from Mayom that I was living in Kibera and that I was trying to resettle in the United States. Jala and I went to Mayom's house to take baths there.

Mabor had worked for NGOs and used to fly to various parts of Sudan, including the capital, Khartoum. So he was immune to the government's oppression and brutality due to the fact he worked for this international agency.

On the day I delivered my photos to him, Mabor tried to talk me out of going to the US. "Why do you want to go there?" he asked.

"I am going there for better opportunities and a better life," I said.

We were having that discussion at Mayom Athien's house, in Uwungumu estate in Nairobi. Mabor tried to convince me to stay in a refugee camp in Kenya until the war in Sudan was over and then I could go back to my hometown of Rumbek and live with my siblings. I could tell from his expression that he didn't want me to go to America.

Most people, especially our elders and those who were not educated, were skeptical about our resettlement to the US. They were afraid of the unknown, especially that the US appeared to be bringing over only young men. They thought we weren't ever going to come back to Africa.

"I am going there for better opportunities," I told my Uncle Mabor. "Sudan is now at war, and nobody knows when it is going to end. There is not much education in the refugee camp. It is better for me to go the US, because I can get a better education there, and I can work and have some money. Maybe in the future, I may reunite with my siblings."

Based on what I had heard from immigration personnel, when I got to the United States I would be able to sponsor my brother, sisters, mother, and cousins to follow me there. I knew that information and so relayed that to my uncle. I could tell by his eyes that Mabor was not convinced. Neither of us was able to change the viewpoint of the other. We shook hands and parted.

Mabor traveled to Sudan and gave my photos to my mom and siblings.

Years later, when we were reunited, my youngest sibling, Martha, said when she first saw my photos, she wept and did not want to look at them. She didn't believe that the guy in the picture was really me, because I was so malnourished, like a prisoner in a concentration camp, or somebody who suffered from chronic tuberculosis or HIV/AIDS. My other siblings, Mary and Peter, said they didn't know what to say because they were shocked.

The news about my dad's death was especially sad for me, because my goal was to go to America, get a college education, then return to South Sudan and support him, Mom, and my Aunt Chuot in their old age.

My dad was possibly born in the mid-1940s, one of five children. He went to school late, probably when he was fourteen or fifteen years old. Back then, our people did not value education. When my father was young, families sent bad children to school. When they saw a child who did things well, was well-organized or hard working, that child remained in the camp. If a child was inattentive and let a cow stray too far and it was eaten by a lion or hyena, that child was sent to school.

Educating children cost money many people did not have. If you wanted to send a child to school, he or she needed a uniform, which the family had to buy. The family had to buy books. If the only kid in the family was sent to school, where was the family going to get money? Who was going to work their crops? They'd have to sell a cow. If they had to keep selling cows, they'd become poor and have to pull their kid out of school anyway. If you did not know the value of education, you did not support it. My dad went to school not because he liked it but because he was frustrated being in the cattle camps.

My father was the second oldest, behind my Aunt Chuot Kuandak. He owned a beautiful bull named Marial, a type of color. Even today, for the Dinkas in Southern Sudan, the cow is everything. If there was a drought one year, a person traded a bull for grain. So that year your family survived.

Marial was a very beautiful color, with patches of black in between white. In the cattle camps, young people went around and chanted songs, beautiful ones. All the girls were impressed by my dad's bull. In Dinka culture, an ox to a young man is like a sports or muscle car to a young man in America. The ox is everything. Young men cleaned their bulls by drying cow dung, burning the dung, and rubbing it onto the ox. They manipulated bulls' horns to grow in any style they wanted; they grew in a skewed fashion, sometimes curving off the animal's forehead.

For some reason, my grandpa sold my dad's ox. I do not know why. When my father's bull was sold, that was like a parent in America selling their son's Ford Mustang. It made my father very angry. How was he supposed to impress women? He left and went to a town called Bar Gel, Gel River, northwest of Rumbek where missionaries used to be. The Episcopal Church is dominant in Southern Sudan because of the British. My dad joined the missionary school and started to learn English. According to him, he was tracked down by my grandpa and taken back to the camp a few times, but he kept escaping and going back to school. Eventually, Grandpa gave up.

Missionaries were willing to educate children who were interested in education, so they could use them to spread the importance of education—and Christianity—to their parents and relatives as well. The British provided children with short pants, and allowed them to live in dormitories. My dad learned English there. His family did not have to pay for missionary school because there was no fee. The school took care of that. My dad stayed in the school dormitory, but did not have a bed. He had a mat made of woven coconut leaves. He had a bedsheet, uniform, extra clothing, but no shoes. He eventually went to medical school in Juba, where he studied to become a nurse.

My dad worked as a nurse from when I was born in the 1970s until the war interrupted. The war interrupted everything. My mom never went to school. She lived during a time when girls were not allowed to stay in school for very long, if at all. Back then she was kept in the family to be used for a dowry. She milked cows and provided services. In the rainy season, which is in May, June, and July, the cattle produced a lot of milk.

My dad married very late, probably in his forties. He was so busy studying he did not have time to come home. In Dinka Agar, you do not marry a girl from a family you do not know well. He wanted to finish school before he came back to the village. However, my dad's younger brother, my Uncle Mamer, stayed behind in the cattle camp. He was the one who chose my mom for my dad. He was getting concerned about my dad getting old and not being able to attract a wife, so my uncle checked out the background of my mom's family. Word came back to my dad, so he went to the village and met my mom, and they talked. He went back to school, but my uncle was not going to give up.

My Uncle Mamer stole my mom and took her to where my dad was studying. Her cousins and relatives searched for my mom and could not find her. When you steal somebody's daughter, it's as if you stole his property because daughters bring dowries. They will find the relatives of that person and attack them. My mom's relatives confronted my uncle about her disappearance, and the young adults started a fight with Mamer. Usually, people fight and hurt one another if somebody steals or impregnates a girl. Our people fight with clubs.

Mamer responded that he intended no disrespect, and assured them that they were willing to talk about marriage. He told them his older brother wanted to marry Cholhok. That is my mom's name.

The elders stepped in, and said, "Let's not cause bloodshed." They said, "Malath wants a family. He is a good man. He is educated. He's doing well for the community." They allowed my dad to marry my mom if he paid thirty cows as a dowry. Back then, that was a lot. Therefore, they got married.

I was born on September 25, 1976, in Rumbek, Southern Sudan. According to my parents, my mother was pregnant with me for eleven months instead of the usual nine. I later found out why they thought my mom was pregnant with me for that long. She had never been to school, and she did not know much about the process of becoming pregnant. Probably, she did not know when she had become pregnant with me. I was her first child, and she did not notice me at first. However, to the whole village, it was a miracle. Most people believed that the pregnancy had lasted nearly a year. Some of my closest relatives even believed my mom was pregnant with something besides a baby.

When the day finally arrived for my mother to give birth to me, another miraculous thing stunned everybody. She was in labor for about twenty-four hours. It is ordinary for a woman to give birth in a village in Dinka tradition. There are local midwives who handle the delivery process, but my mom's was an extraordinary one. When the labor lasted for almost a day, there was a concern that she was going to die. Since these midwives faced an unprecedented situation, they had to convince my uncles, aunts, and grandmothers to sacrifice a sheep to Nhalic, a God, so the God could facilitate the delivery.

My dad was at odds with them. He had medical training and knew for sure what was going on. He told them their thinking was all nonsense, and he insisted on taking my mother to the hospital where she finally had a C-section. Had my dad not received the education he had, I bet my mom and I surely would have died. He was able to pinpoint what was going on with my mom and save our lives. Most women in the remote villages die due to delivery complications and the absence of advanced medical care.

Six months later, all of my close relatives got together for my naming ceremony. They slaughtered several sheep and lambs and prepared a big feast. Neighbors and distant relatives who lived far away, about two days' walk, were invited. All kinds of people showed up—children, young adults, men and women, and the elders. The meal consisted of kisra, bread-like food made from whole grain flour, chiaya, steak, ades, lentils, aguot, mung bean, molokhia, a vegetable like spinach cooked with onions, garlic, and meat, and assida, a thick porridge made from ground millet. The way to eat assida is to plunge your fingers into the stodgy mound, scooping out a lump of it, and mopping up some of the sauce. It is served with a sauce made from okra or molokhia. The assida itself has a gritty texture and is filling.

While girls and young women prepared the food, they gave young children some peanuts to keep them from crying so their moms could do the cooking undistracted. To Dinka kids, peanuts and peanut butter are like cookies and ice cream to American children. I remember every morning my mother prepared me milk tea along with either makuanga, peanut butter, or roasted peanuts. Any day I got neither of them was a bad day for me. For instance, when I herded goats and sheep, if any of them went missing, my mom punished me by not giving me peanuts the next morning.

After the feast was served and everybody ate to their full satisfaction, people danced. Elders were then served mauher, a beer made from grain flour, and aragie, hard alcohol similar to vodka; also made from grain.

In Dinka culture, young people do not drink alcohol until their children are married and have their own families. At that time, they are considered successful in life. Therefore, they can enjoy the rest of their lives to the fullest. Parents are highly respected and appreciated by their children for focusing on raising them properly rather than buying alcohol to support their own pleasure. After the children have grown up, parents have the freedom to live in any child's house and can move to other kids' houses any time they wish.

While people danced, my dad, mom, uncles, aunts, and grandmothers gathered in the house where they had privacy to debate what would be my permanent name. Before the naming ceremony, I was being called by all kinds of names. Some used to call me Poth, survivor, Taban, suffering, and Marial, the color pattern of the ox that my dad had paid as dowry when he married my mom. Marial is very beautiful and one of the recognized colors in Dinka. As previously noted, a Dinka man who possesses an ox of Marial among his cattle attracts many girls. When he finds a girl that he likes, he sings songs that extol the beauty of that young girl, but also the songs praise the magnificence of the ox.

Those who gave me the above-mentioned names insisted that one of those should be the formal name for me. The debate dragged on and on for hours. Finally, my Aunt Chuot Kuandak, my dad's older sister, grew tired of the prolonged argument, and said, "Stop bickering! This child will be called Ater."

In the naming process, the father always has the final say about what name should be permanent. Other relatives may make suggestions, but if the father does not like the names being proposed, he can come up with his own and everybody respects that as the formal name. My dad liked the name "Ater." That was why he didn't object to my aunt proposing it. Other names are not ruled out completely. They are still used in informal occasions. Even now, my brother and sisters and other relatives still call me "Taban."

Ater has several meanings in Dinka. It means bickering over trivial matters, which was what my aunt intended when she silenced the argument at the naming ceremony. Another meaning is deadlock. For instance, when two individuals have a dispute, which they cannot resolve. The expression, we are like oil and water would be a better analogy to illustrate the second meaning. Finally, Ater means perseverance. Later on when I was growing up, that type of personality attribute manifested itself in everything I did.

Whether I was working on a farm or facing a bigger boy who bullied me at school, I never quit or backed down. Even though a bigger boy beat me up, I'd keep fighting back until he'd get tired of me and ran away. At that point, I'd become the winner and loser at the same time. Other boys chose whether to declare me a winner or a loser. Those who hung out with me automatically called me a winner, but deep down inside, I knew I had lost, but I always refused to acknowledge the defeat. That was when others came to understand that I was well-named as Ater, due to my perserverance. My father noticed as well and later thanked my Aunt Chuot for coming up with the name of Ater.

In the years ahead, in a new land and facing a new culture, I would need all the perserverance my name foretold.

ATER MALATH

Chapter 19

Flight to the United States

Jala and I flew to the United States on September 24, 1995. I was nineteen years old. It had been ten years since my uncle and I had been forced to flee our village. I had survived many hardships. Now I embarked on a new journey for a better life.

Khamis' flight to the United States had departed two weeks before ours, and he was sent to Fargo, North Dakota, where my cousin, and Khamis' friend, Deng lived.

Jala and I went to Nairobi's Jomo Kenyatta International Airport at 7:30 p.m. At about eight p.m. our plane took off. My stomach churned up and down due to nervousness, but I was able to control it. I had had a similar experience before, on the helicopter from Tiragol to Itang. The Boeing 747 airplane we were on was huge! Even though I had flown in a helicopter before to the refugee camp, this aircraft was much bigger and flew at a higher altitude. It had beautiful seats, and we watched TV.

On the KLM flight, all I could think of were the things I wanted to accomplish once I got to the US, such as getting a good education and the possibility of reuniting with my relatives in the future. I was also planning to work hard to save up some money, and one day when Southern Sudan became free, I would go back there and start up a small business. I was concerned about the amount of culture shock I was sure to experience in a new country.

Everything on the plane was written in English. I could tell there were Sudanese refugees who didn't know how to read or who didn't understand English. They took salt and put it into tea. Or they spread sugar on their food. I could read labels and instructions so avoided those mishaps.

On board, the flight attendants served beverages. I had Heineken. Service was not frequent. They gave us one can of beer each and waited for about forty-five minutes before serving us another.

"Please, may I have some beer?" I asked a flight attendant.

"Sorry, it's not time yet," the flight attendant replied.

It was very frustrating. While they held off serving beer to Sudanese refugees I saw other passengers being served it. I thought they were discriminating against us. We later found out that on the flight before ours, people got beer whenever they asked for it, but some refugees became drunk and acted inappropriately toward the flight attendants. Because of that, the attendants cut down on the amount of beer served to refugees.

Our flight landed in New York City the following morning. We walked out of the terminal to catch a bus to the hotel the INS had booked for us. One group of people from our plane walked ahead of us. Following them were two white guys, Lual, and me, and then a last group. All of us walked toward an automatic sliding glass door.

When the door slid open, it frightened a group of refugees, who had never before seen such technology. They ran, and then everybody, including the two white American men, ran in different directions. The white men probably thought somebody was going to shoot people. They didn't know it was the sliding door. Jala and I ran too. I thought somebody was going to open fire on us. After the door closed once again, some of us came back, stopped, and stared at the door like sheep that had been scared by hyenas.

When the two American guys realized the refugees were scared by the sliding door, they came back and went through it. The group of refugees watched them as they passed through, to make sure nothing bad happened. Jala told me, "Let's go, man. It's just a sliding door." We went through and then everybody followed us.

The bus came on time and transported all of us refugees to a hotel, and we ate breakfast there. We could order any kind of food we wanted, except beer. Some refugees argued with the hotel restaurant manager because we weren't served any, even though other restaurant patrons were being given it. One refugee confronted the manager and demanded beer. He said, "What happened? We need beer. We need beer."

The manager replied politely, "I'm really sorry. We can't serve you alcohol because INS has not paid for it. If you guys have some money, I will serve you beer. There is no other reason I can't provide you with beer."

After we finished eating, we went to our rooms. That was my first time sleeping in a well-furnished room. I said to myself, *Now, I am really in America. I am no longer in the Kibera Slum.*

The phone in the room rang. I jumped out of bed and picked it up. It was there all along, but I didn't know what to do with it until it rang. I said, "Hello, who is this?"

"It's me, Lual," he said.

We talked in Dinka. "Eka de?" (How are you?) He enquired how I was feeling about being in America and staying in a nice room like that. I told him that I was feeling very good.

It was then that I reflected upon the life I had gone through, walking hundreds of miles, living in refugee camps, often hungry and never entirely sure I was safe. Then to the many challenges of Nairobi and living in the Kibera Slum.

When I was living in the refugee camps or in Kibera, I simply accepted those places as my home. I thought back to the noise, stench of feces, and filth of Kibera, and said to myself, *You know, it was so bad where I was living. I was living in a very dirty place.*

Looking around that nice hotel room, with my own phone, in the United States, I realized I had indeed come a long way.

Chapter 20

New Life in the United States

The following morning, Lual and I went to the airport for our final destinations. I was going to Fargo, North Dakota, and he was going to Seattle, Washington. Lual was sent to Seattle by Ronald, the INS attorney who had interviewed the Sudanese in the Ifo refugee camp. Ronald was so appreciative of how Lual had served Sudanese refugees by being a translator and how he had facilitated their jobs as well. As a result, he wanted to pay him back by sending him to a state with a nice climate, and so he chose Seattle as an ideal place for Lual to live because it doesn't snow much there.

I was sent to Fargo because my cousin, Deng, went there in 1994. The INS wanted to minimize culture shock as much as possible and figured the best way to do that was to send newly arrived immigrants to cities where they had relatives.

Unfortunately, before I arrived, Deng had moved from Fargo to Sioux Falls, South Dakota. Later on, he told me the reason he had moved to South Dakota was that he had heard from a religious organization called Lutheran Social Services, LSS, that I was sent to a different state. Whenever refugees were admitted to the United States, the INS worked with organizations such as the International Rescue Committee, IRC, and faith-based groups such as LSS as sponsors to facilitate the accommodation of newly arrived refugees. LSS sponsored Deng back in

1994, and it was the same church-based organization that sponsored us again in 1995.

I arrived in Fargo on September 25, 1995. The weather was very nice. It was in the lower seventies. I landed at Fargo International Airport at three p.m., but once in the airport saw neither Khamis nor Deng. Eventually, I spotted a white woman approaching me.

At that moment, many things swirled in my mind. I recalled the woman in Nairobi who suspected I was being brought into slavery in America. I didn't see any of my own people. I was alone. I had been told that when I got to Fargo my cousin, Deng, would be there to receive me. Instead, this white woman came toward me. I carried an IOM plastic bag, which contained all my documents. In addition, I had on my nametag. As soon as she was about to get close to me, I stepped back a few meters to give myself some space, pretending as if I didn't see her.

She called my name, "Ater, I am your case worker. My name is Susan."

At first, I didn't believe her, anxious that this was part of some plan that would make me her slave.

She said, "Khamis is here with me."

Then I saw Khamis and all my fear vanished. I shook hands with them. After that I was taken to the place where three other Sudanese immigrants lived—John Mukhtar, Muhammad Nyanmele, and Mahmud. We lived in a two-bedroom and one-bathroom apartment. I lived in one room with Muhammad Nyanmele, and John Mukhtar and Mahmud were in the other. The apartment building was three stories. Mostly immigrants from Vietnam and China lived there.

The next day, Susan came and took me to the welfare office. I filled out a form and received some assistance. I was given food stamps and cash for nonfood items, such as toothpaste, toilet paper, and laundry detergent.

North Dakota was such a new experience for me; totally different than anything I had known before. Fargo, even though it's not as big as many other metropolitan cities, was big in my eyes. My first problem in North Dakota was finding addresses. All the buildings looked the same to me. The first few days I'd ride my bicycle a couple of blocks and then back, unsure where to go.

The weather remained mild through to the end of September, and we played soccer, volleyball, and went biking. We Sudanese have a dark complexion compared to African Americans. People could tell we were from a different country and sometimes asked.

One day, while I was riding my bike, a guy pulled over his Chevy Blazer and asked me, "Where are you from?"

I said I was from Sudan.

"What made you come to this nasty state?" the man asked.

"What's wrong with this place?" I said. "Look how nice the weather is."

"Wait, let October come," he replied, but did not elaborate. He gave me his business card and told me that I should call him in case I needed any help. I can't remember what type of business he had because I was new in the country and didn't know the importance of it.

On October 10th, my caseworker came over, and said: "Ater, we are going shopping for winter clothing."

I asked her, "How bad is the winter here?"

She replied, "It snows a lot and gets really cold here in North Dakota."

I instantly recalled the Chevy Blazer man's comment about October and realized he referred to bad weather when he said to me, "Wait, let October come."

Susan took me to a place where refugees were given free winter clothing. When I got there, I met a lot of refugees from Sudan and many other countries as well. I was given a long coat, snow boots, a hat, and gloves. I thought to myself, *What the hell is going to happen?* I couldn't imagine a winter as bad as those heavy clothes indicated.

The woman who gave out the items told me winter was coming soon and that we had to be prepared for it. I was very worried.

On October 15th, approximately fifteen inches of snow fell. It did not seem that cold at first. Kids ran out of the apartments to play in it. I went into my room, opened the window, and watched what was going on. That was my first time seeing snow in person. I had seen pictures in geography books, like snow on Mount Kilimanjaro, but I had never physically touched it. About thirty minutes later, I mustered up the courage to go outside. It wasn't cold.

To me the snow felt like ugali flour that I used to cook in the Kibera Slum. It felt coarse. The kids made snowballs and threw them at one another. It was a very nice day. However, two days later, the temperature plummeted. At that point, being in Fargo was like a death sentence to me. I was used to a warm climate, but now all I had to do every day was battle subzero temperatures.

Early on, transportation was a major challenge. I didn't have a car to get around. I needed a friend who had one so he could get me to the places I was eager to visit. Even going shopping was a big problem for us. My roommates and I were fortunate to live close to the grocery store, Sunmart. Once a week, all three of us walked to the store, which was about two blocks away, purchased everything we needed that week and then walked home.

To go to places such as Wal-Mart, we had to call a cab. Because we often were so bored, we'd listen to tapes of Congolese and Kikuyu music, as well as the Dinka tapes that we had brought with us from Africa. Even though we spoke neither Congolese nor Kikuyu, we enjoyed listening to the beat because we had been exposed to that music during our stay in Kenya. Every day John, Mahmud, and me rode our bikes to the park and played basketball or soccer. Thank God the Lutheran Social Services provided us with those bikes. It would have been much harder for us to get around on foot.

Early on, I became convinced it was necessary for me to embrace my new country, my new home, with open arms. I wanted to meet somebody who could take me to places like churches, nightclubs, bars, or malls so I could meet people and make friends and learn American culture. I had been dropped into this new one. I had no choice but to accept it as my second. I have my own, but this one also was mine since I live in the US. Because we were new in the city, we didn't know places where we could go for fun. Of course I had a caseworker, Susan, who used to take me to the hospital for doctor's appointments or to the welfare office, but those places weren't much fun.

During my second week in Fargo, I met my first friend, Paul. He was in his mid-forties and was married to a Japanese woman. They had a six-year-old daughter and a nine-year-old son.

One afternoon while we were playing basketball at the park, Paul pulled over in his car and enquired where we were from. We introduced ourselves to him and exchanged phone numbers. Every weekend, he invited us to his church. He belonged to the Unification Church founded by Reverend Moon. The first time he invited us, only Mahmud and I agreed to go with him, but my other roommates, John and Sunday, politely declined the invitation by saying they were busy trying to call their friends in Nairobi. Later on, they told us they did not make any phone calls; it was just an excuse—they just didn't want to go to Paul's church. The second week, Mahmud stopped going, but I continued accompanying Paul. I knew nobody would force me to become a member.

It all depended on me. As I said earlier, my main goal was to learn the culture, and that meant getting involved with people.

Sometimes, Paul's wife prepared dinner and asked him to pick me up to eat with them. Paul once told me that he had found his wife through an arranged marriage by the Unification Church. He suggested I should get married to an Asian girl through the same process as well, but I politely replied that I wasn't interested.

Paul was the person in Fargo who initially made me feel at home. My association with him and his family eased me into American culture. One afternoon, Paul notched up our interaction by inviting me to his son's hockey game. Once we got there, I found out something very extraordinary—they played hockey on ice.

We Dinka have been playing hockey for over a thousand years. Our hockey, adiir, is played on the bare ground. We designate an area as a goal. It can be a tree or a mere circle drawn on the ground. In the past, our people made the puck from tree sap or wood. Nowadays, it's cut out of a tire. People hit it with a crooked stick to the goal, and the opposing team hit it back to the other team's goal. Another big difference I noticed between American hockey and adiir is that we don't wear any protective equipment such as helmets, shoes, or goggles. People occasionally got hurt by a flying puck. The worst injuries happened when one hit a person in the eye or genitalia. When we played adiir against other boys in the village, I'd watch out for the puck in case it came in directly at eye level or at the groin. If it did, I'd use my bare hand to protect myself or simply dodge it. Adiir is more dangerous than American hockey, but the concept is the same.

During the halftime break, Paul took me to the concession stand to get us something to eat. He asked, "Ater, what would you like to eat?"

I didn't know what kind of food to order. Paul went on to explain every kind of food on the menu. He said, "They have hamburgers, corndogs, hotdogs, popcorn, and pizza."

I asked, "What are you going to eat?"

He answered, "I am going to eat a hot dog."

I told him I'd like pizza. I didn't want any food with the word "dog." Really, I thought those hot dogs and corn dogs contained dog meat.

After we were done eating, we went back in for the second half of the game. Unfortunately, we found out that our seats had been taken so we had to look for different ones. As we walked around, I noticed some kids pinching on cotton and eating it. "What are these kids eating, Paul? Why are the children eating cotton? Why don't the parents stop them from eating it?"

Upon hearing those comments, Paul burst into laughter, and said, "Ater, it is cotton candy. It's not actual cotton, but it's made to look exactly like cotton. Would you like to try it?"

I said, "Yeah, of course I want to taste it." He asked one of the kids if he could have some, and the kid agreed. Paul pinched a handful of cotton candy and handed it to me. When I put it into my mouth, it simply dissolved immediately, but it tasted sweet, just like candy.

Unfortunately, Paul's son's team lost the game that evening. After it was over, we went back to his house. On the way home, the conversation was about the game, mainly between Paul and his son. Paul praised his son's performance and pointed out the areas where he needed improvement.

I sat there quietly as if I wasn't there at all, thinking about the hot dog that Paul ate at the concession stand. After we got home, I asked him, "Paul, I'm curious, what's hot dog made of?"

He replied, "Oh, it's made of beef. Why?"

"I thought they are made of dog meat since the name has something to do with dog," I said.

Paul said, "No, Ater, they're actually good. You should try one someday. You might like it."

Chapter 21

First Job in America—Meat Packing Plant

After two months on welfare, my caseworker, Susan, came in a van in the afternoon, picked me up, and took me to a meat packing plant to apply for employment. The plant was a combination slaughterhouse and meat processing departments. It was located nearly three miles from the city. A quarter a mile before we reached the plant, a stinky odor engulfed our vehicle, so I rolled up the window. I couldn't make sense of what it was.

I asked, "What smells like this?"

"We're about to get to where the beef is processed," Susan explained. "I guess that's where this smell is coming from."

"Is that where I'm going to apply?"

"Yeah, we will try applying there first, because if they hire you, it's okay, but if they don't we will go and apply to some other places. I think a lot of immigrants work here. Therefore, they should be able to hire you as well."

I believe Susan meant for me to get a job there because she knew there weren't many employers interested in hiring unskilled immigrants, other than the meat processing plant, because of immigrants' inability to communicate effectively with native speakers in English.

In America, immigrants face many obstacles with employment, in addition to language barriers. Unskilled immigrants are recruited for jobs that often are disgusting, back-breaking, or mind-numbingly tedious. This processing plant needed workers desperately because most Americans refuse to take the dirty jobs of butchering cows. So a lot of their workers were immigrants who couldn't speak English very well. The company hired immigrants from Eastern Europe, such as Russia, Bosnia, and Kosovo, and from Africa and South America, mostly from Mexico, and a few Vietnamese. Some Americans held all the management positions.

Although I was grateful I had employment and could earn money, I didn't like the job; however, I felt I had no choice but to take it. We went to the company employment office. I filled out an application and turned it in right away. Three days later, I was called for an interview.

I came in, and the manager asked me basic stuff such as, "Can you lift seventy-five pounds of weight? Can you work twelves hours a day?"

I said, "Yes, I can."

He asked me whether I used banned drugs, such as ecstasy, cocaine, heroin, or marijuana.

I said, "No, sir, I don't."

"Okay, come in tomorrow and I will take you to your supervisor," he told me.

I came back the next day and reported to the manager. He called Dick, the supervisor of the boning department, on the phone to come and get me. Dick provided me with white aprons, a helmet, metal chains that you wore underneath the apron like a bulletproof vest, arm guards, knives, a hook, sharpener, gloves, and steel-toed shoes. I felt like a soldier being equipped to go to war.

The key to being an outstanding employee at the boning department was being able to sharpen a knife and keep up with your assigned part of the carcass. If an employee was not good at sharpening a knife, he couldn't keep up. It would become so blunt it wouldn't cut the meat at all. There were employees who were so good at sharpening theirs that they were asked to help slackers like me.

Early on, sharpening a knife was a big problem for me. My supervisor taught me how to do it so many times, but I couldn't get it. Once we started the shift, the conveyer belt ran at full speed nonstop until break or lunchtime. As a result, I missed my sections of the carcasses, the hind leg, and the supervisor yelled at me, "Get the damn meat. Don't let it pass you and slow down the line."

The supervisor went down the line and collected sections of the carcasses that I had missed and piled them beside me. It got to the point where he ran out of space. Then he'd fill a barrel. When it was time for break, he told me, "You are not going anywhere until you finish those piles." He made me work on them during my break time, except at lunch time.

Since I was tall and muscular, the supervisor decided to capitalize on my physical strength and height. He led me to where I took halves of cows off hooks as soon as they came out of the cooler. I next pushed them down the line where other workers chopped the meat to pieces. The half cows weighed about a 150 pounds each.

Meat processing began right after the slaughtering department killed all the cows that were scheduled to be processed that day. First, the cows were brought in trucks and kept in a fence for several hours, which calmed them down before they were sent to the slaughterhouse. They drove them through dark, winding corridors, which were also designed to keep them calm. The cows came up on the conveyer belt. Their heads popped out and a worker called the knocker shot six-inch bolts into them, killing them instantly. The death process took a minute so the cows didn't feel pain or sensation at all. However, I felt it was still a brutal and undignified way of killing cattle.

Their bodies were washed right away to prevent the spread of diseases like e-coli. They hung them on huge hooks by their hind legs and removed the hides, hooves, heads, and guts. Nothing from the cow was thrown away. Every part went to a different department. After those parts of the carcasses had been removed, they used a giant saw to split them into equal halves from the neck all the way through the backbone.

They were pushed into a giant cooler where they were inspected by USDA personnel. After they had been approved, they were pushed to our department, boning, for processing. That was where my job kicked in. I removed halves of cows off the giant hooks where they were hung. I stepped on the machine with my right foot so it lay flat, placed the cow on the surface, and pushed it down the line. I did this day in and day out.

Within two months of working there, I started gaining weight and kept gaining. I weighed more than 200 pounds. I think that was what helped me cope with that tough job. I was eating a lot, and it immediately turned into muscles because I was working out lifting cow meat. That job was like exercise to me. I ate a lot of food, but after a few hours of working, I'd feel hungry once again because the job was so physically demanding.

The supervisors set the temperature around twenty-five degrees Fahrenheit to prevent the meat from spoiling. In spite of the cold, I still sweated as I worked. A mist often formed inside my helmet, and then I couldn't see a person at a distance of five meters away due to poor visibility.

The work space floor was very disgusting. All over, it was covered with blood mixed with pieces of meat and water. The first week of working there, I couldn't stand the smell and lost my appetite. I went home and just stared at food, because when I pictured the stuff at work, I just felt like puking. Eventually, I got used to it.

The supervisors treated us like prisoners. They ran about hustling everybody in the line. They frequently yelled at us, "Move, move, let's go." We couldn't stretch because the moment an employee paused for a few seconds, a supervisor yelled at him.

What kept us going through the hard work of the meat processing plant was the time a group of us Sudanese shared during lunch break. At lunch, we occupied a table and ate there as a group. Each person warmed up his food and then brought it to where we sat. Once it was set on the table, it no longer belonged to you; it belonged to the group. Once we started eating, you could grab any food that tasted delicious to you and eat it. Most of the time, I didn't get to eat my own food, and I felt good that my friends enjoyed it.

In my department, there were about seven Sudanese, apart from my three roommates—John Mukhtar, Muhammad Nyanmele, and Mahmud. Mahmud was six foot five inches tall and worked harder than most people in the department. He was quiet but had a friendly nature. Mahmud used his stature to help other workers lift down packages from the tallest shelves and still was able to keep up with his own tasks.

Muhammad was about five foot eight with a fairer shade of skin and made up for Mahmud's silence by talking all the time. Muhammed and Mahmud were from the Dinka tribe. Muhammed was daring and was the first of my group of friends who bought a car, a Hyundai. He wrecked it within five days of purchasing it from an auto dealership named JD Byrider.

I wanted to buy a car because my friends and roommates were all doing so, but Muhammed told me, "Ater, don't buy a car right away. Save your money, learn to drive well. Otherwise you will just crash it like me!"

Every weekend we got together outside work and had a party, either at other Sudanese friends' apartments or at our place. All the Sudanese people in Fargo knew one another by appearance. Although

I didn't know each one by name, I knew most by sight. We Sudanese are collectivists. We like to socialize and hang out in a group. You don't have to be invited to a party to show up there. All you have to do whenever you're bored is pick up a phone and call your friends to make sure they're at home and then join them. We considered it a sign of popularity if many people wanted to hang out with you. It meant you had a good reputation. Most of the time, I showed up at my friends' doors and started knocking.

That kind of close association we had enabled us to deal with stressful situations effectively. For instance, at the meat processing plant, the emotional support we used to give to one another during lunch breaks helped us cope with that strenuous work. Whenever I felt down, didn't want to talk to anybody, and came to the lunchroom in a cranky mood, at least one or two fellow Sudanese encouraged me to be positive. As a result, I forgot all the unsettling images and thoughts that wandered around in my mind. Although I deeply missed my parents, the cohesiveness of our community helped at least partly fill that void in me.

Apart from small parties that we used to go to on a weekly basis, we also met at other major events, such as Christmas, New Year's Day, and Sudanese Memorial Day, which we celebrate on May 16th to honor our brothers and sisters who died in the Sudanese conflict. Sometimes, when we got off work early, Mahmud and I went to the park and played either volleyball or basketball.

Another reason our community was so close was a powerful communality—the war in Sudan. It had displaced all of us from various parts of Sudan to America. That was the key element that sustained the cohesiveness among us. Despite the fact we had tribal disputes back home, which were encouraged by the regime in Khartoum, we considered ourselves in America as Sudanese regardless of our tribal backgrounds.

Before the civil war broke out, all the tribal strife was based on territory for cattle. From the mid-1980s on, as civil unrest became intense in the south, the government of Sudan became actively involved in exacerbating the existing tribal disputes. The government put tribes against each other, and even launched its own militias, such as the Murahaleen or Janjaweed, who traveled on horses all the way from the north to the south to massacre villages in Dinka territories.

The meat processing plant paid very low wages. I started out at $6.30 per hour. Our grotesque jobs were by no means equivalent to the pay. We got up very early in the morning and worked a twelve-hour shift until late in the evening. If they slaughtered 900 cows on a given day, we considered that light, and we went home as early as three o'clock. More typically, they killed about 1,500 cows per day. I was amazed at how many they slaughtered, but Americans—and the whole world, for that matter—like to eat a lot of meat. According to the US Department of Agriculture, about 32 million head of cattle are slaughtered in the United States every year. That is processed into about 25 billion pounds of meat. That is a lot of meat, and a lot of slaughtered cattle!

When they killed 1,500 cows in a day, we'd work from six a.m. to six p.m. My whole body was constantly sore because I was not used to that sort of extremely strenuous work.

Most refugees didn't own cars, so Lutheran Social Services hired an Asian guy to drive their van to get us to work. We paid $50 a month. In the morning, he drove around collecting people and dropping them off at their workplaces.

During the first week on the job, a problem occurred. I forgot to turn on my alarm clock. I overslept and missed the van as a result. The van came and honked the horn, but unfortunately, I didn't hear it. So the driver left and dropped off the other guys. The line didn't start in our boning department because I wasn't there on time to lift the cows. Due to my absence, some supervisors were doing my job instead.

My supervisor called me, and I heard my phone ring loudly. I picked it up, and said, "Hello."

"What are you doing?" I heard.

I said, "Who is this?"

"This is Dick, your supervisor."

Dick weighed over 250 pounds and had a humongous beer belly. The guy also had a very bad temper. Whenever something upset him, he was in a bad mood all day like a hungry lion. He again said to me, "What are you doing?"

"Oh, I missed the van," I said.

"You fucking call a cab," he said.

"What is the cab?" I didn't know what a cab was because all I knew was a taxi. I had never heard a taxi called a cab.

"Call a fucking taxi!" he demanded. I told him that I didn't know how to call a taxi.

He said, "I am going to call it for you. Give me your fucking address and get your fucking ass in front of the door right now. If you miss the cab, I am going to fire you."

The guy cursed me badly. As I went outside to wait for the taxi, I thought to myself, *Is this how life in America is going to be like?* I was also thinking about what Dick had said—that if I missed the cab again he was going to "fire" me. Because he was so mad at me for being late to work, I thought he might shoot me. I thought when somebody said "fire" he meant shoot. I later learned that firing from work meant termination of employment. We don't use that word in Africa. We use words like expel or dismiss. The term of fire was incomprehensible to me based on the context used by my supervisor.

I wondered why Dick was so furious. I got into the cab, went to work, and began doing my job.

After sixty days, I demanded a raise. I told my supervisor that I needed one; otherwise I would quit. He called me into his office, and said, "Ater, you are a good employee. You are going to get a raise." I got a one-dollar raise. He said I was doing a great job and that was why I was given it. If I had been doing a sloppy one, I probably would have been fired for asking for a raise.

Lying in bed after coming home from work, I'd ask myself, *Is this what I came to America for, to be a butcher? I could have done this job in Africa because we Dinkas raise cattle.*

I'd tell myself, *No, I won't settle for this kind of job.* I worked twelve hours a day, and when I got home, I ate and went to English as a Second Language, ESL, classes in the evenings. I didn't take it as a bad thing to do that kind of job, but I used it as motivation to learn more so I could move up the economic ladder. Some of my friends said, "Oh, we are tired; we can't go to class today." I'd say to myself, *If I keep telling myself I am tired, but with this job, I am always tired, when will I not be tired?*

Chapter 22

Pride of my First Car and a Mishap

Through work, I was able to save up $2,500 and sent it to my cousin, Deng, in Sioux Falls to buy me a car. He bought a 1991 Eagle Summit with 45,000 miles on it for $6,500. He drove it to Fargo and then trained me for three days before he went back to South Dakota.

Me (in jeans shirt) with friends in front of my first car- Blue Eagle Summit

In the winter of 1996, I was taking ESL classes, to which the Lutheran Church provided transportation. One day, at the last minute, we were informed that the van was not going to be able to take us to class. I didn't want to miss it because I believed improving my English was the only way out of my job at the meat processing plant. Since I couldn't find another ride on such short notice, my last resort was to drive my own car. It was 5:30 p.m. and rush hour in Fargo when

I struggled with the decision on how to get to the ESL class. I had a driver's permit but no formal driving instruction—only three days of training from my cousin.

Before going, I was very indecisive, faced with a big dilemma about whether or not I should drive. A big struggle was going on within me. One voice said I shouldn't drive because I hadn't yet received enough training. It cared about the value of a human life, very concerned about me killing innocent people because of my driving inexperience. Then, there was the other, self-centered voice, which was blind to the consequences of endangering other peoples' lives and focused solely on my self-interested goal of getting to the ESL class. I was placed in a judge's position by those voices and had to come up with a decision. The one, which would benefit me, could potentially cause damage in lives and materials to other motorists on the road, but not driving would leave me without the education I needed. I stood by my car for a good five minutes, listening to that internal debate.

Eventually, I said to myself that it was only a one-time thing. I was going to drive that day, and when I got back from the school, I'd park the car until I got a license and insurance. I immediately jumped into my car and started driving. Immense nervousness instantly overwhelmed me. I started sweating profusely as soon as I sat in the driver seat. My main problem was moving my foot from the gas pedal to the brake and vice versa. If I just kept my foot on the gas, I was able to drive perfectly fine until either I came to a stop sign or a traffic light, where I had to move my foot from the gas to the brake. I had a tendency of trying to look at my foot every time I changed from the gas to brake pedal.

One of my Sudanese neighbors named Meja rode with me. He was my coworker at the meat packing plant and went to the same school for advanced ESL classes. His car had engine problems that day. Afterward,

I could not believe I did not see the simple solution of letting Meja drive my car since he had a driver's license and had been driving for a while.

While I drove to my ESL class, as I approached each traffic light, I silently prayed it would remain or turn green so I didn't have to worry about changing my foot from gas to brake. Meja wasn't aware of the tremendous stress I was going through. He thought I knew what I was doing so he was just enjoying the ride. I had become an expert at controlling my feelings. I was always calm and composed when it came to stressful situations. So Meja didn't notice what was going on with me.

There was another emotion at work in me—I was immensely proud of owning my own car. I had never thought I was going to own one in my lifetime. When I was growing up in Rumbek, only rich people could afford cars. Even my dad, who was a nurse, never had a car. He rode a bicycle to work. Being in America gave me the opportunity to experience what it felt like to be rich in my country. I wanted to experience that feeling by actually driving it myself.

Five blocks away from my destination, the school, that pride of owning a car turned into a nightmare. The traffic light turned red as soon as I was about to make a left turn and I had to stop immediately. For some reason, probably panic, my foot slid from the brake to the gas pedal and as a result, I hit a Ford SUV that was in front of me. The trailer hitch behind the SUV bumper pierced through the front bumper of my small Eagle Summit.

I was very angry, because to me it was like one of my own family members had been injured. This was the car that I loved so dearly, and suddenly its front had been damaged and looked very ugly. At first, I irrationally thought the driver of the SUV was the cause of the accident. That occurred to me, but then I told myself, *No, no, no, Ater, not in America.* I realized I needed to deal with the consequences of my own actions and not engage in scapegoating. I was the one who hit his car; he didn't back up and hit mine.

I stepped on the brake and put the car into Reverse so I could back it up a little bit, but my foot stayed too long on the gas and my car backed into the car behind me. It was a big mess. My friend promptly put the car into Neutral and finally into Park. I was sweating profusely because I was worried about getting a ticket and possibly being sued by the other motorist.

I looked through the windshield to see whether the guy in the SUV had suffered any injuries. The first thing I noticed was that he moved his head in a circular motion and at the same time feeling his neck with both hands. I was afraid he had suffered a neck injury. Within a few seconds, he got out of his car and came to mine. I was relieved to see him walking just fine.

The first question he asked me was, "Sir, do you have insurance?"

I said no.

He asked, "Do you have a license?"

I replied, "No, sir, I don't have that either."

He shook his head and backed away from my car, looking very disappointed.

Back in 1995, there weren't cell phones around. In order to make a phone call away from home, we had to use a pay phone. There weren't any public phones near the scene of the accident so he asked two young girls who played in their backyard to call the police for us.

I didn't want to get out of my car because I was so embarrassed. Bystanders were hanging around and kept staring at me. I asked myself, *What's wrong with these people? Why don't they leave me alone and mind their own business? Do they really think I did this on purpose?* I worried that those people thought I was a hardheaded guy who came from another country and didn't want to abide by American laws. Of course that was pretty much accurate. Legally, I was breaking the law by driving without a license and insurance.

Where I was growing up, I had never witnessed any car accidents because there were so few cars in Rumbek, especially compared to Fargo and America. My hometown was a small one then. I could ride a bike around the town and literally count all the cars. Most people who owned them there didn't need insurance. So when I came to Fargo and got my first car, it didn't click in my mind the importance of car insurance. I thought it wasn't a big deal. To me, paying for it was like throwing money away. In fact, I didn't really have a full understanding of traffic laws when I got my permit because my reading level wasn't that good at that time. I memorized key points of the informational pamphlet to enable me to pass the test and get a learner's permit.

About five minutes after the accident, police arrived at the scene. The officer asked me the same question the SUV guy had asked me earlier. "Sir, may I see a proof of insurance, registration, and license please?"

"No, sir, I have none of them, except a permit," I replied.

He enquired, "Where are you from?"

I said to him that I was from Sudan.

He asked me again, "Don't you know that it's illegal to drive without insurance and a license in the state of North Dakota?"

I said, "Yeah, I know."

"Then why are you driving if you know that it's against the law?" he inquired.

I replied that I didn't have a choice but to drive.

I explained to him that I worked twelve hours a day, seven days a week, butchering cattle. I said that I was new to the country, and I was trying to settle in. I wanted to improve my English so I could get a better job. I explained to the officer that in my hometown being a butcher is the lowest of all jobs, but now I was cutting meat every day in America. I didn't want to do it for the rest of my life, so that was what motivated me to drive to school without insurance and a license. My ride wasn't going to come, and I didn't want to miss the class. I told him that I was going to drive that day, park it when I got home from school, and never drive it again until I got insurance and a license.

After I was done relating my story, he looked at me for a while, and said, "Mr. Malath, I won't allow you to drive on from here. Do you know anybody who we could call so he could drive your car home? If you can't find anybody, I will have it towed."

My friend, Meja, who rode with me, suggested to the officer that he would drive my car home. The officer agreed to that idea, and said, "Wait, a minute, I am going to talk to the other driver in the SUV, and I will get back to you in a minute."

I don't know what they talked about, but the next thing I saw was the SUV guy driving away. I told myself, *Oh, my God, my world is done now.* I thought they had cooked up something against me since both of them were white, and now I was going to pay a heavy price.

Instead, the officer showed some compassion for my plight.

"Mr. Malath, I am not going to give you a ticket since it's your car that has been badly damaged," the officer said. "I am going to give you my card and you must call me within two weeks and at least give me proof of liability insurance. In two months, you must call me again, saying you have a driver's license. From now on, don't drive until you have fulfilled these requirements. Otherwise I will give you a big ticket and impound your car for good."

My friend, Meja, drove my car to school and back home. The following day I went and got liability insurance and called the police officer to let him know I had complied with his orders. When I took my car to the mechanic to get him to assess how much it was going to cost me to fix the front bumper, he said $500, including parts and labor. I had wondered why the officer didn't give me a ticket. Now I knew—he realized I was going to pay a heavy price for my action one way or the other. I appreciated the fact that he didn't give me a ticket on top of having to pay for repairs.

Two months later, I called the officer again to let him know I now had a driver's license and I had fulfilled all his requirements. He thanked me for obeying his orders and advised me to be careful on the road. I should not have driven to school that day and should have listened to the ethical voice in me, which didn't want me to drive in the first place. I acted selfishly by not listening to my conscience because my immediate needs got in the way of my rational judgment.

Chapter 23

Fargo Winter. Time to Leave

I arrived in Fargo in September 1995. The winter of 1996 was very severe. At one point, a severe blizzard lasted throughout the night. The snow fell so fast that when dawn arrived, there were eighteen inches of snow on the ground. I couldn't believe what I was seeing! The only cars on the road were government trucks, plowing and dropping sand. Other than that, there was no one in the streets, neighborhoods, or parks. The whole city looked like a town that had been evacuated. The wind whistled through the empty streets. It reminded me of the Sudanese town of Rumbek when the SPLA, Sudan People's Liberation Army, attacked the army garrisons, and all the civilians fled for the day to avoid crossfire.

The Department of Transportation put out a weather advisory that no one should travel unless there was an emergency. They said the temperature was forty below zero, including wind chill, and the wind was blowing nearly seventy miles an hour. All the businesses were shut down for two days. Throughout all those days I was snowed in, and I felt as if I was in jail. It was too cold for anybody to go out. If you did, you had to bundle up like somebody in Antarctica. It was painfully cold.

Before that, I had only known a hot climate with a rainy season and a mild winter. Back in Sudan, we lit a fire and sat around it, sipping black tea when the temperature dropped to what we regarded as a cold sixty-five degrees. Those were the coldest days I had ever known, and the Fargo winter was a new shocking reality, which I had never expected.

Having lived through one severe Fargo winter, I was determined to leave for somewhere warmer before the next one arrived. It was incomprehensible to me why the immigration department would send people from such a warm climate as Sudan to such a terribly cold place as the state of North Dakota. I later learned that many places in the United States have a climate similar to South Sudan; for instance, Florida and Arizona. If the immigration officials hoped that I was going to adapt to that frozen environment, then I must have disappointed them. By the summer of 1996, I realized I didn't want to live through another Fargo winter and was determined to leave.

At that time, I didn't know what states to go to because I hadn't done any research. I called my cousin, Deng, in Sioux Falls. I informed him about my decision to leave Fargo before another winter came and my desire to find another job. It was too cold, and the meat processing plant was my only option for work in Fargo.

He said, "Wait! I'm going to come to Fargo so we can talk about it." He did not have a job in Sioux Falls and also was looking to move somewhere else.

When Deng showed up in Fargo, he suggested we should go to Nashville, Tennessee, because he knew some friends there. Friends of his had told him about the city, the mild weather, and the jobs available there. They said there were a lot of opportunities for temporary work that could become permanent if you worked hard. When he proposed moving to Nashville, I depended entirely on him since he had come to the US before me and knew more about the various parts of the country.

Since I had just finished paying off my car, I didn't have money for traveling to Nashville. I suggested to Deng that we find summer jobs other than the meat processing plant so we could save some money before traveling. The meat processing plant was too physically demanding for me, and at the same time, I was sick and tired of working with meat, especially in cold temperatures, and the smell was bad enough to even keep the visits of USDA inspectors very short.

Clearly, our decision to move to Nashville wasn't only for the nice weather but also for jobs. In Fargo, the meat processing plant was the only company that used to hire the majority of immigrants. If you quit working there, it was extremely hard to find another job. However, we heard from friends that there were many jobs in Nashville. Therefore, we agreed to look for summer jobs in Pelican Rapids, Minnesota, which was a thirty-minute drive from Fargo, so we could save enough money to get to Nashville.

Pelican Rapids is a small town with one gas station, one Laundromat, two banks, and one traffic light. Very rural. That place was small, but the work was much better than in Fargo. We applied for work at the turkey plant. James Malek, a Dinka friend of mine, worked there. He informed me that employees worked in a warm environment.

I had known Malek since the Kakuma refugee camp in Kenya, but he initially was sent to Washington D.C. He moved to Fargo to find a job, but ended up working at the meat processing plant as well. He worked there for a few weeks and quit because he couldn't handle the cold.

I told him, "Malek, if that company is like the meat processing plant, forget it, I will not work there."

"No, no, there is a packaging department. There are different kinds of jobs that you can do. You can do cleaning at night if you like," Malek said.

Based on that recommendation, my cousin, Deng, and I went to Pelican Rapids and rented an apartment near the turkey plant.

The way turkeys are processed is cleaner than with beef. Trucks traveled out to farms in the countryside and crews loaded live turkeys into cages and brought them back to the plant for processing. Other people removed them from the cages and hung them by their necks in a specially designed conveyer metal fitting for the turkeys' necks. This metal choked them right away. You could see the birds dangling and flapping their wings before their last gasps. Then the conveyer proceeded to a container full of hot water and submerged them in order to loosen the feathers.

The turkeys passed through a narrow passage where the feathers were removed by big hoses that blew strong currents of air onto them with the help of big, flat objects that looked like cut tires, which slapped the turkeys as they passed by them. After the feathers had been removed completely, the turkeys were rinsed clean and chopped up. The fat was removed and the meat was ground up and cooked to make all kinds of products. From there it was packaged and prepared for shipping. The process was much warmer overall, and there was no bad smell.

I liked that job better than the meat processing plant, but I had no intention of staying there longer than necessary. We were just saving money to get to Nashville.

The turkey plant was better. The birds are smaller than cows, so it wasn't physically demanding like when I had to take heavy cows off hooks. When we first moved to Pelican Rapids, my cousin and I were in the shipping department. We packed the deli meats into boxes for shipping. We'd also take them out of the machine that cooked them. It was really hot. We'd shrink wrap them and then pack them. I worked helping pick up turkeys from farms. For the farm job I went with the truck drivers. We, the loaders, had a small pickup truck with a conveyor and lift. We followed the trucks to farms that had huge buildings with thousands of turkeys.

Workers pushed the turkeys through onto the conveyor belt. Once they came down the conveyor belt, we took them off and put them into the cages in the trucks. Once the lower cages were full, the lift moved up with us. The turkeys were heavy; some weighted sixty-five pounds. You had to be careful or they'd scratch you or try to fly off. Once the turkeys arrived at the plant, workers pulled them from the cages and placed them into the conveyer metal fittings by their necks, beginning their deaths and processing.

Although the turkey plant was easier work than the meat processing plant in Fargo, I was dismayed by the manner which livestock were killed at both plants. I had never seen such a mass killing of cows and birds in my life, where the animals struggled as they died. To me, it was like a massacre, the idea that cows were slaughtered in hundreds and turkeys in thousands. I bet if those turkeys could talk, they would have complained about the inhumane way in which they were murdered.

In South Sudan, I had seen livestock killed, but not in such a mechanized, sterile way. A family might slaughter a goat, sheep, or chicken for the purpose of consumption for a meal or a feast. For whatever reason it might be, the animal was laid on the ground in a dignified way before its throat was slit. Some people held front legs and hind legs and somebody held its mouth. If it was a chicken, only one person slaughtered it. You laid the chicken down facing east, stepped on its legs with your right foot, held the head with its eyes completely covered with your left hand, and then slit the throat with your right hand.

We worked at the turkey plant during May, June, and July. In mid August, we quit our jobs. We rented a U-Haul truck and left for Nashville, towing my Eagle Summit. We left Pelican Rapids at six p.m. to go to South Dakota so Deng could say goodbye to his friends there before we moved south. It took us about five hours instead of the usual four to get to Sioux Falls, and we spent the night there at my cousin's friend's apartment.

We arrived in Sioux Falls at around eleven p.m. We stopped at a McDonald's and ate some Big Macs and french fries before we got into town because we were hungry and exhausted from loading stuff into the truck and driving. We ate at McDonald's because we thought Deng's friend might wake up in the middle of the night when we got home and feel compelled out of hospitality to prepare us something to eat. We didn't want to spoil his sleep. When we got there, we were given a mattress, so Deng let me sleep on that in the living room while he slept on the couch. We slept until noon. We ate a lunch, consisting of steamed rice and baked chicken with some pinto beans.

We resumed our trip at around four p.m. I was the first to drive because I am not comfortable driving at night. During the daytime, I can drive up to twelve hours without any problem, but at night, I can only last for a few hours. I like to be able to enjoy the terrain I am driving through. If I can't see anything in my surroundings and just narrowly focus my view on the road illuminated by headlights, I feel bored and sleepy. Deng is one of those nocturnal drivers. He likes nighttime driving. Deng suggested I drive first for at least two or three hours, and if I felt sleepy, I should let him know so he could take over. I managed to drive for six hours.

The truck we rented had a top speed of sixty mph. It was a very slow drive. I was concerned about the truck; it was a dingy, rickety-looking vehicle. The engine made a strange *tat-tat* sound. I worried it might break down before we got to Nashville. Deng was confident and assured me it would get us to our destination, though he conceded it would be a grueling trip.

I said, "Maybe that white man at the U-Haul might have given us this truck on purpose."

Deng disagreed, and said, "No, it was tough luck on us. He didn't intend to do this to us. Don't worry, Ater, it will take us to Nashville." Deng had been driving for almost three years. I guess that was why he was more confident about the truck. In contrast, I wasn't up to his level yet because I had never driven on an Interstate prior to our trip.

Every little noise from a car freaked me out. There was one point in Fargo when I took my car to a mechanic and asked him to check the engine because it wasn't running well. The first thing he told me was that he couldn't figure out what was wrong with the car by just looking at the engine. He suggested that if I really wanted to find out what was wrong with it, he could perform a diagnostic test. He did it, but found nothing wrong. However, I had to pay $45 for the diagnostic test anyway. I was so ignorant when it came to cars back then.

On our way to Nashville, there were places where the posted speed limit would be seventy mph, but we couldn't drive that fast. All the other cars and trucks zoomed past us. We couldn't tell where we were by just looking at the street signs.

It was such a long, boring trip. There is not much to see on Interstate highways on that route. National Public Radio, NPR, filled in the gap. I like NPR very much. It brings unbiased news from around the world. To me, NPR is like the BBC in the US. I listened to all kinds of programs such as *Talk of the Nations, All Things Considered, Science Friday, To the Point*, and business news and so on. At one point, Deng and I listened to the BBC on NPR and the topic was the rapid rate that technology was accelerating and changing. It was said five to ten years from then, 1995, a bachelor's degree would not be a guarantee to middle class status. The radio report said it was necessary for young people to keep educating themselves so they could keep up with the pace of technology.

On hearing that news, I was very concerned about my future in America. Getting a bachelor's degree within that timeframe discussed on NPR seemed as unattainable to me as traveling to Mars. Having just emigrated to the US from a war-torn country, with no formal education or even a high school diploma, and speaking very little English, I feared it would take me longer than ten years to get a college degree.

It was scary to hear such a disturbing piece of information while still new in the country. I realized that if I didn't do anything to better my life in this land of opportunity, then I likely would stagnate. On the other hand, it was a wake-up call, because hearing that information early during my life in America eventually motivated me to be proactive in getting an education.

I learned from other refugees from underdeveloped countries like Sudan that it can take years just for basic transition to a new culture, including finding a job and surviving in a new land. Deng and I talked about the possibility that Nashville could be the place where we'd fulfill our hopes of finding better jobs. I was eager to find a better one, finish ESL classes, and start taking the General Educational Development, GED, test to get my High School Equivalency Diploma so I could go to college.

Clearly, my resettlement to the United States wasn't over when I landed at Fargo International Airport. It was an arduous process for us, the first Sudanese immigrants who came in 1994 and 1995. We had few people to turn to for help. We were pioneers to other Sudanese who later came to the US. We had to figure things out through experience, but the downside of that was it took time. We had to learn everything from scratch without support from family members.

Back home in Dinka culture, it's all about "us" and "ours." Because we are a collectivist culture, we share everything. Whenever a family member brings in something—whether it is food, such as a sack of grain, or money—it automatically belongs to everybody the moment it reaches home. That process does not focus solely on the material things that are contributed to the family, but the day-to-day living issues that each family member encounters. When one faces a problem, everybody does whatever he or she can in order to help out, to the point where that burden is spread out. However, in the US, I had to deal with all my problems by myself. It was very hard and stressful adjusting to life in America. It meant finding an ideal climate, a good job, learning English, and so forth. That was why I spent the first few years in the US travelling from state to state, trying to figure out where I fit in.

It was a big switch for me from living in a collectivist culture to an individualist one. When I came to the individualistic culture of the US, where everything depends entirely on one's own ability, I found it hard. I had no one to turn to for assistance, such as parents, brothers, or sisters.

Back in the Ifo refugee camp, I knew America was the land of opportunities, but when I arrived in Fargo, I realized I had to work hard for them. Some people had worked very hard in the past for the many freedoms we are enjoying today in America. The same thing applies to our day-to-day lives. I am glad I had figured out early what it took to succeed in America. For instance, the meat packing plant position that I did in Fargo wasn't the job of my choice. I didn't come to America to butcher cows. I could have done that in Sudan. However, because of the language barrier, I took it on temporarily, knowing I would have to learn English to get a better job. It was a very hard one, but because I needed a car, I couldn't wait until I got a job that I liked. I had to do it.

Chapter 24

Nashville

We arrived in Nashville the next day. It had been a very tiring trip in that slow truck. We were exhausted and hungry, as though we had been walking on foot for a day. We parked the U-Haul truck at a Kroger grocery store parking lot, went in, and bought some fried chicken and coffee to wake up. As we walked to the store, I heard some people talking in an African American accent, but when I looked to confirm what I had heared, I saw a white police officer questioning a black man.

"Is this officer imitating the black person's accent?" I asked Deng.

"No, he is not," Deng said, explaining that was how people talked in that region of America. "Both whites and blacks talk like that. This is down South, my friend. You're no longer in Fargo or Pelican Rapids."

After eating, we drove to the apartment that we had booked by phone, not far from Kroger and Murfreesboro Road, the main street in downtown Nashville. It had two bedrooms, two bathrooms, and cost $650 a month. It was a medium-range price and a very clean apartment.

One thing that I didn't like right away was the traffic in Nashville. There were cars everywhere. It was rush hour so everybody raced home from work. What made it worse was the loud music that many people listened to in their vehicles. It wasn't as if they just listened to it so they could enjoy it in their own cars. People had huge speakers in their trunks, and when they listened to the music they liked, they raised the volume very high and at the same time rolled down the windows. It was noisy everywhere and distracting. Having been used to a smaller city like Fargo and the very rural Pelican Rapids, Nashville was overwhelming, so big and full of life.

My biggest problem was getting around. Learning local streets was not easy. I was okay driving to the grocery story, about five to six blocks away, but whenever we wanted to go farther out to look for jobs, I let Deng do the driving. I was worried about getting lost, but also about other motorists running into me. People in Nashville drove more crazily than Fargo, and I wasn't used to that.

One thing I did like about Nashville was our proximity to the grocery store and the downtown area. Our balcony overlooked the Murfreesboro road, giving us a nice view of the shopping center and the main street. In the evening, Deng and I sat there and watched the activity going on in the streets. We settled into our new place and then went around looking for jobs.

Even though the economy was very good during the Clinton Administration, it was very hard to get hired directly. We were told by our friends there that the quickest way to get hired was to interview with temporary agencies, and then they found you a job that fit your skills and ability.

We went to the temporary agency office and filled out application forms. They told us when to come in again. In two to three business days, they called us, and said, "We have found some jobs for you. These jobs are temporary. If the employer likes your performance, he or she may keep you."

In my opinion, temporary agencies used people instead of helping them find permanent jobs. They went around and made contact with business people who often needed unskilled workers, like Deng and I.

During that temporary period before the employer decided whether or not to keep us, our paychecks went through the temp agency. If my pay rate was $10 an hour, for example, the temp agency would take $3.50, leaving me with $6.50. I didn't know exactly how much they deducted from my paychecks. I'm just giving an example to illustrate what was going on back then because the temp agencies never told us what amount they took from our paychecks. All I used to see on mine was my hourly rate, gross, and net pay.

The temp agency people claimed they made deals with companies to find them workers and, as a result, they got paid for doing that. However, one time when I tried to apply directly to a company I was told I wasn't going to be hired unless I went through the temp agency. It was a win-win situation for temp agencies and business people.

Business people didn't have to offer employees benefits such as health insurance or raises, and temp agencies made money off temp workers. Businesses could keep employees for two weeks, three weeks, a month or two months, then let them go and hire a new batch of temp employees from temp agencies. Either way both parties took advantage of us. They shuffled us like playing cards. I had jobs for a few weeks and then was laid off. Then the temp agency called me again, offering another temp job. I'd start all over again. I worked so many temp jobs I can't remember most of them. The only job I can clearly recall was packing magazines, a job I held for sixty days.

When I was in Nashville, I wasn't connected with other people of different nationalities. I used to hang out with Sudanese, mostly Dinkas. Some people went to nightclubs, but I did not. I heard those could be dangerous, especially if you hung out with the wrong people.

After a while, I suggested to Deng that temporary jobs were not a long-term solution. "Let's work during the day and go to school in the evenings," I suggested.

That was where we disagreed. Deng told me that we were too old for school. At that time, we were in our early twenties. He said, "It would be a good idea for us to just focus on working. In the future, if possible, we could sponsor some kids from Sudan to come to America so they could pursue education." I told him I wasn't too old for education and started taking advanced ESL classes to prepare me for GED classes.

A few weeks later, Deng came up with an idea. He said, "Ater, these jobs do not pay well. I'm not going to waste my time. I'm going to attend trucking school." I asked him whether he was going to drive locally and be able to pay his share of rent. After he finished truck-driving school, he said that was his intention.

So, Deng started his truck driving training in a small town about a thirty-five-minute drive from Nashville. The school rented him a motel room during his two weeks of training. He ran out of pocket money. So he called me up and asked me to loan him some. I was still staying in the apartment. I drove in my Eagle Summit from Nashville to where he stayed in order to bring him $125.

I jumped onto a highway at about four p.m., rush hour. At the time, I was still new to driving. I saw an empty lane so I switched over to it. I felt much smarter than other motorists who were stuck in slow-moving traffic in the other lanes. What I did not realize was that I was driving on an HOV lane, in which there had to be two or more occupants in the vehicle. I drove on it for about fifteen minutes; then I saw a state trooper behind me. He didn't turn on the flashing police light so I continued. He followed me for quite a distance. I thought, well, if he didn't turn on his light, probably I'm fine. He and I were the only people in that lane. In fact, if I had been a more experienced driver, upon seeing him behind me, I likely should have left the HOV lane. All of a sudden, I saw four police cars ahead of me and the whole highway got shut down just because of me. I looked back and saw his police light flashing. I asked myself, *What happened now?*

Police swarmed my car. They ordered, "Get out of the car." They searched me as well as my car but didn't find any weapon. I was given a $347 ticket for driving in the HOV lane and having a dim brake light. They told me to get the hell out of the HOV lane immediately, and not to drive on the HOV lane again if I did not have a passenger on board.

When I arrived at the motel where my cousin stayed, I gave him $125 and told him I had gotten a very big ticket on my way there. He said, "Don't worry about it. If I get on the road and start driving, I will help you to clear it off your record."

After he was done with the truck driving course, Deng came home one night and informed me that he was going to drive Interstate. I asked him, "You said before that you were going to be driving locally and be able to pay your share of the rent."

"The company requires me to drive interstate," he said.

"What about the rent? How am I going to be able to pay $650 rent while you know I get paid $6.35 per hour?" I asked.

"When I get on the road, I will be sending you my share of the rent through MoneyGram," Deng said.

"That would be great if you could do that," I replied.

He sent me his share of rent for October only. We still had three more months to pay—November, December, and January. Lack of money became a major concern, and I wasn't able to attend classes. After some time, Deng called me. He was in Sioux Falls, staying with his Sudanese ex-girlfriend. I took advantage of that opportunity and told him that I was thinking of leaving Nashville.

In December 1997, two Dinka guys, Juug and Bol Maming, came from the Job Corps in Batesville, Mississippi to Nashville for Christmas. I knew Juug from the refugee camp back in Ethiopia. Before they showed up, I had entertained the idea of attending Job Corps someday, but did not know enough about it to make an informed decision before then.

Fortunately, Juug and Bol came to celebrate Christmas with us in Nashville. I invited them to my apartment and explained my situation. "Look, I used to go to school in order to get my GED, but now I'm busy working two jobs to pay the rent. The jobs are not stable either because every now and then I get laid off. What do you think about me joining you at the Batesville Job Corps? Do you think I could get my GED there?" That was my last resort. If they hadn't come to Nashville, I likely would never have earned my GED.

Juug said, "Ater, I would recommend that you come to Job Corps because it's a government-sponsored program. It provides an opportunity for low-income families' children who dropped out of high school to get their GEDs and trades and get back on track with their lives. We eat three meals a day. We have all kinds of recreational activities that you can get involved in. We have a weight room, basketball program, volleyball, and free movie trips to Memphis, Tennessee, three times a week. Job Corps is the ideal place for you if you need to get a GED. When your apartment lease expires, you should join us."

I was relieved to hear that welcome information. They showed me the Job Corps office in downtown Nashville and told me to apply there after the Christmas holiday was over. We celebrated Christmas together, and they returned to Job Corps.

Chapter 25

Batesville Job Corps (Now Finch-Henry)

After Christmas of 1997, I applied at the Job Corps office in downtown Nashville as instructed by my friends, Juug and Bol. In January 1998, two weeks before the lease expired, I called Deng in Sioux Falls, South Dakota, to inform him that I was going to attend Batesville Job Corps in Mississippi. I still had my Eagle Summit and some of his clothing was in the master bedroom of the apartment. I said I wanted him to come before I left for the Job Corps and to take the car along with all his belongings.

"Ater, where are you leaving me? Where do you think I'm going stay?" Deng asked.

"I want to get my GED, but life here in Nashville is not conducive to education because I work two jobs just to pay rent and bills," I said. "As a result, I am unable to attend ESL classes anymore. I heard that Job Corps provides free GED classes, training for a trade, and accommodations. I am going there to take advantage of that opportunity. Furthermore, my license has been suspended because I did not have money to pay for it. So if you think you're not going to make it before I leave, let me know ahead of time so I can sell everything in the apartment, including my car, and pay off the ticket that I got when I delivered the money to you at the motel."

Deng said, "Wait, I will come there." He traveled to Nashville, took all his clothing, packed it into my small car, and drove back to Sioux

Falls. I gave away the furniture, cleaned the carpet, and handed over the keys to the landlord.

On February 2, 1998, I took a Greyhound bus to Job Corps. The school paid for the bus fare. We left Nashville at six p.m. and stopped for a while in Memphis. In Memphis, I saw some people who were as dark as I am. I thought all African Americans were light skinned. I smiled big because it was very exciting to see black people who were a hundred percent black like me.

I went to a nearby convenience store, bought some potato chips, orange juice, and a bottle of Aquafina, and then went back to the station. The majority of the passengers were blacks. I sat there eating my chips, analyzing the features, such as noses, mouths, and faces, and tried to relate them to some of the African tribes I knew of, including my own, the Dinka.

A few minutes later, our bus took off. We stopped at Montgomery, Alabama, then Jackson, Misissippi, before reaching Batesville Job Corps. Now I realized I truly was in the Deep South. Everywhere I looked I saw four out of five people were blacks. I had lived mainly among white people in Fargo so did not have the opportunity to learn African American culture. There were not many of them in Fargo. I became so excited now that I had the opportunity to live with them and be able to learn their culture and traditions. One thing I noticed as I travelled to Job Corps was that the blacks' accent was a challenge for me to understand.

We arrived in Batesville around two in the morning. I was picked up at the Greyhound bus station, along with other newly arrived students, by a Job Corps van. The Greyhound bus station was a few minutes away from the school. We were searched for weapons at the main gate of Job Corps and then led to the male dorm. I had three roommates—Alex from the Virgin Islands and two African Americans, Dave and another boy. I cannot recall his name.

The entire Job Corps center complex was fenced. It had four dorms, two for males and the other two for females. Batesville Job Corps was comprised of nearly three hundred male and female students, of whom ninety-nine percent were African Americans.

Every Tuesday new students came to Job Corps, and that's when the staff put new arrivals through orientation. During that, staff talked to us about different trades we could explore to determine what we were interested in. They also talked to us about things we could not do. Despite the fact that numerous students joined the school every week, many left after violating a zero-tolerance policy for drugs, alcohol, and violent behaviors.

Job Corps is a great program that helps a lot of people. It was started during the 1960s as part of President Lyndon Johnson's efforts to eradicate poverty and was modeled after the Civilian Conservation Corps, which put people to work during the 1930s Great Depression. It is seriously committed to offering students a secure and safe environment conducive to education. Therefore, students who violate this policy are dismissed immediately. The orientation allowed me to see clearly the opportunities Job Corps could offer me. It enabled me to set my goals, and pushed me to take advantage of those opportunities.

On a typical day, I got up as early as six a.m., ate breakfast, and spent the majority of my day receiving academic and hands-on career technical training. After classes, I studied or hung out with friends before dinner in the cafeteria. Mostly I played pool at the recreation center or watched TV. Sometimes, if I had no chores to do at the dorm, I went to the weight room and lifted weights. We went to bed by ten p.m.

However, during my first week at Job Corps I felt extremely out of place. Everything was different—the way people talked, walked, and dressed.

One day that week, we talked about something in our room when Dave, my roommate, kept telling me, "Hey, dog, chill out, dog."

I was deeply insulted. Angry, I grabbed Dave by the collar.

"Don't ever call me a dog, okay," I shouted. "I am not a dog. In my culture, if you call somebody a dog, it's a big problem."

"I'm not cursing you, dog," Dave said, continuing to call me a "dog."

I pushed him back into a corner and tried to choke him. One of our roommates ran to the RA and reported that I was beating up Dave. It was a physical mismatch. I am six feet two inches tall and then weighed 200 pounds; Dave was about five feet and two inches tall and weighed about 165 pounds.

The RA asked me, "Why are you beating up people, Ater? What happened?"

"This guy called me a dog. If he doesn't stop calling me a dog, I will beat him up," I said, shaking with anger, pounding the table with my fist at the same time.

She pulled me aside to talk to me separately, trying to defuse the tension as much as possible.

"Ater, I know you're mad and you have the right to be furious, but you're in Mississippi," the RA patiently explained. "The way we talk here is different, but it doesn't mean anything bad at all. It doesn't mean that someone is insulting you on purpose or does not like you. Our young people around here talk this way. What Dave meant by 'dog' was simply saying 'What's up, man?'"

"No, he didn't say that," I insisted.

"That is slang for 'What's up, man?'"

At first, I did not believe her. In my mind, I thought she was on Dave's side since they both were African Americans and I was an immigrant from Sudan.

However, I kept hearing people greeting one another by saying "What's up, dog?" at the cafeteria, the gym, and even in classes. Now, I realized Dave did not insult me by telling me "Chill out, dog." I began to accept it as a way people talked, just as the RA had told me, and from there on I used it to greet other students. At first, I felt nervous calling people "dog," but whenever I said it to someone, that person always responded positively so I kept using it.

When I first arrived in Job Corps, I was given a placement test to determine which classes I needed to take. I passed a math placement test so I was placed in an actual GED math class. I spent two months in the GED math class and, when I felt confident, took the actual GED exam for math and passed it. I was then left with the other four subjects that I had.

Mr. Hudson reading class – 1998

My reading level was very low, so I failed a placement test for Interpreting Literature and the Arts, Writing Skills, Social Studies, and

Science. In order to get to the GED classes for the remaining subjects, I had to take a reading course. Job Corps had a program called Step Out Reading, from level one up to level six. My English instructor was Mr. Hudson, an African American. I worked hard. I did in-class assignments and asked him for extra homework and books to read. I started out in level two and worked my way up to level six. After stepping out of reading, I was allowed to enroll in GED classes for the rest of the subjects. It took me almost a year to get my GED. I enrolled in the Job Corps program on February 2, 1998, and received my GED in December.

While I was working on my GED, I was also taking a trade course. At first, I went into auto mechanics for three months. However, the instructor did not teach but let students work on the cars they brought in for repair. He believed in giving us primarily experiential knowledge. He only intervened to show us something that we could not figure out how to fix. His strategy of hands-on training indeed worked for students who had some prior knowledge of working on vehicles. I did not have any so his strategy did not help me at all. Just to learn the basics of mechanics took more than what it took other students.

When I realized I was not getting it, I talked with the instructor to see if I could switch to a different trade. Job Corps allows students to list three trades of interest. My choices were auto mechanics, printing press, and welding. When I talked to the instructor, he told me that I could switch to my second choice, but switching to another trade after three months into auto mechanics training would prolong my stay at Job Corps. I told him, "I don't care how long it's going to take me. The important thing to me is that I like a trade."

I talked with the principal in order to get enrolled in lithographic printing. After I received my GED, I concentrated on my trade. The printing press was much easier and more understandable than auto mechanics. The instructor taught us a lesson. Then after that, we practiced what we had just learned on presses. We printed forms, fliers, business cards, and so forth. After six months, I was sent to Ole Miss University on a school-to-work program for a month, where I worked closely with experienced print press operators as a way to hone my skills before graduating and getting back into the labor market.

We received paid allowances—approximately $46 after tax—twice a month for nonfood items, such as toothpaste and a toothbrush. We kept some of our allowance as pocket money so when we went to the movie in Memphis, we'd be able to buy some snacks. We had student's accounts where the school kept track of how much each student had in theirs.

Every month, the school conducted a general evaluation of each student's performance. The school sent evaluation forms to all instructors, who then reported back to the principal on student performance. The instructors gave points based on academics, trade, and even social interaction with other students. Through those points, a student could either get bonuses or not. Every month, I got a bonus. When I graduated in July 1999, I had $2,700 in my account.

After I obtained my GED and a diploma in lithographic printing, the school principal, Mr. Wyckoff, recommended I continue at Job Corps and go to community college. The college program had many benefits, such as academic advising, mentoring, tutoring, paid tuition fees, books and supplies, housing and recreation, and transportation to and from the college of your choice. Batesville Job Corps had a van that transported students from Job Corps to community college in the morning and back to Job Corps in the evening.

"Ater, it would be a good idea to get your AA degree from the community college while you're still here, because if you leave Job Corps now, you're going to face a lot of distractions," Mr. Wykoff said.

While the principal appeared to be offering good advice, I think he made such recommendations because many students did not continue their education after Job Corps. I was confident I was not going to be distracted after I got out of Job Corps. I deeply appreciated the opportunities this country provided me.

"Here, the school is paying for everything. All we need from you is to be passionate about your education so you can have a bright future. We don't want you to leave Job Corps and still work a low-paying job," the principal told me.

I told him I would think over his suggestion.

The truth is that I was fed up with the environment at Job Corps. While the education, food, and other benefits were great, I did not like the social life.

Job Corps was like a voluntary prison to me. Job Corps had security guards who patrolled the center day and night. We were not allowed to drink in the center. We could talk to girls, but that was it. The way to go out with a girl was to apply for a written pass. When it was approved, then you could rent a motel room and have fun there over the weekend. Going to a motel was costly as we depended on the allowances—$46 every two weeks after taxes—given to us by the school.

Some boys sneaked into the girls' dorm to make love with their girlfriends and girls vice versa. I was too old to engage in that kind of activity; more appropriate for teenagers instead of an older student like me. I was almost twenty-two years old. It was very risky—a student caught doing that by a security guard could be dismissed from the program and sent home for good. I did not want to be dismissed before I received my GED and a trade. I was more desperate for an education than girls.

There continued to be cultural differences that were hard for me to endure for much longer. Many students came from poor families, were poorly educated, and had personal issues, including drug problems. A lot were profoundly ignorant about other cultures, especially Africa. They asked me stupid and embarrassing questions, such as, "Do you guys have deodorants in Africa? Do you go naked like those we watch on TV? Do you have cars?" I endured those rude and shallow-minded questions because I knew where they were coming from and I needed my GED and trade.

When I was asked an ignorant question, I thought to myself, *Do not worry about these comments because if they, these children, were smart, they would not be in Job Corps in the first place. They would have gotten their high school diplomas and gone to a good university.*

One day I talked to my English instructor, Mr. Hudson, about the stupid questions students asked me. He told me not to think too much about the negative comments others made about me because they were not that educated about their own country, let alone other continents, such as Africa. He told me, "To prove what I'm telling you, I'm going to ask one of the students who are the president and vice president of the United States, but I bet you he or she won't come up with the right answer." The student whom he asked knew only Clinton, but he did not know Al Gore was the vice president.

For many of the students who came to Job Corps, the restrictions must have seemed like a Marine Corps boot camp. Job Corps officials were strict with us because they knew we had to follow rules in order to succeed. Many students responded to that as though they were being mistreated and rebelled against that authority. Every week, I watched as new students came in and saw many of them wash out, either quitting or being expelled by the school.

Many Batesville Job Corps students, especialy those who gave up and quit, really did not appreciate the opportunities for education they had in America. Instead of quitting or getting expelled they could have been trained in appropriate behaviors and job skills that are conducive to success in the labor market and life in general. When they quit Job Corps, I wondered what other options they had left. For most, I guessed Job Corps was their best chance to get a GED, trained in a trade, and have good jobs or proceed to colleges.

To me, dropping out of school was like giving up. From my struggles in Africa, I could clearly see education was an equalizer, a great path to success in America, and that education, unlike Africa, was so available to Americans, even poor Americans. I came to the realization that a big reason kids in America did not realize how fortunate they were and the opportunities they had was because they didn't have a basis of comparison.

I often told my rommates and friends at Job Corps that they had everything they needed to succeed. They just had to work hard and apply themselves.

"You don't even realize what you have your hands on. You are like somebody who is sitting on gold but is not aware there is gold underneath him," I told them. "When I was growing up in South Sudan, I did not have opportunities such as the ones you have here in America. I woke up early in the morning, walked a mile and a half barefoot to school, and back again in the evening. When I got home from school, I put my books away and took the goats and sheep to grazing until six p.m. I used to dream of light to do my homework that I did not have time to do during the day. The only thing we had was a kerosene lamp, but sometimes we ran out of kerosene."

When my roommates heard my story, their attitudes changed about Job Corps and they became more appreciative of being in it and passionate about their dreams. All my roommates managed to stay at Job Corps until they got their GEDs and training in a trade.

Chapter 26

Rochester, Minnesota, Then on to Seattle

Remaining at Job Corps for another year after I received my GED and trade training in order to go to community college, as recommended by the principal, was out of the question. I thought leaving Job Corps was an opportunity to enjoy a short break before I started community college.

In December 1999, after graduation, Job Corps awarded me $2,700 and a free airline ticket, so I flew from Mississippi to Rochester, Minnesota, where Deng lived. The $2,700 award resulted from my performance at school. It came from academic and trade performance. In addition, social interaction with fellow students, the ability to get along with other people, earned me some bonuses. In Job Corps, I was an honor roll student and that too earned me some bonuses. All those added up. That was how I ended up getting a $2,700 check.

My flight to Rochester was at ten a.m. We had to go to Minneapolis first, then take another plane to Rochester. Early on, when our plane took off, it was cloudy, but by the time we came closer to Minnesota, it became sunny. I looked down through the window and saw everywhere covered with snow. Even though it was warm and cozy on the plane, I knew on the ground it was bitterly cold. Seeing snow brought up into my mind the memories of Fargo winter, the snow, blizzards, and frigid cold weather.

Sitting next to my right was a man who appeared to be in his late forties. He asked me, "Where are you from?"

"I'm from Sudan," I said.

"Where are you heading?" he inquired.

"I have just graduated from Job Corps in Batesville, Mississippi, and I'm heading to Rochester, Minnesota."

"Are you going to live there or just visiting?" he asked.

"Oh no, I'm not planning to stay there. My cousin lives there, but we're thinking of moving either to Atlanta, Georgia, or Seattle, Washington, because I don't like the snow and cold."

"That's nice. Seattle is not as bad as Minnesota," he said.

That man lived in Minneapolis, but had been on a business trip and now he was heading back home. He told me Rochester was a small town and there weren't that many job opportunities there because the two major employers were the Mayo Clinic and IBM, and you had to have some sort of advanced skills to get hired; otherwise, you ended up doing unskilled work, such as a janitorial job.

We arrived in Minneapolis at noon. I spent four hours at the airport because of some delay in the schedule. At four p.m., we were told the flight to Rochester should arrive in a few minutes, but it showed up at five p.m. Finally, our flight for Rochester left Minneapolis and arrived at Rochester at about six p.m.

It was freezing cold in Rochester—about twenty-five degrees; a big change from the Deep South. Akot Cuie, Deng's roommate, picked me up at the airport in Deng's black Ford Ranger. When I reached Deng and Akot's home, I met Deng's uncle, Gum Benjamin, and his Somali girlfriend, Fatuma, who were in the living room. Gum and his girlfriend had just moved to Rochester from Washington D.C. and stayed there temporarily. Deng and Akot were living in a three-bedroom and two-bathroom duplex. I think they probably anticipated many people were coming to stay with them and that was why they had rented that big place. We hung out in the living room for a while. I went to bed because I was exhausted from my trip.

In the morning, Deng and I talked about which state to move to, but he asked me to wait because he wanted to go for a short trip to Missouri; after he got back, then we would talk about it. His trip to Missouri became a tour of three places—Missouri, Nashville, and Atlanta.

Soon after I arrived in Rochester, I had to look for a job so I could help pay bills. I went and applied for employment at IBM. I had heard from other Sudanese who worked there that it was hiring for unskilled positions.

I applied for employment at many companies, but never got a single call from any of them. The Mayo Clinic hired as well but I needed to have some kind of skills to be employed there. The only job I possibly could get at the Mayo Clinic was a janitorial one. I also applied at a small printing company because that was what I had learned at Job Corps, but they too never called me back. Fortunately, IBM hired me. Because I didn't have computer skills, they hired me as a machine operator. They trained me for a week on how to operate a machine to clean computer discs. I loaded the discs into the slots in the machine and pressed a button. The upper part of the machine, which looked like the turret of a military tank, came and fit perfectly on the lower part, poured water onto the discs, and washed and polished them simultaneously.

That machine was easy to operate, but its downside was it shattered the discs in a blink of an eye. I had to keep a close eye on it and, as soon as I heard a weird sound, I pressed an emergency button so it did not damage all the discs. After the machine was finished washing and polishing them, I removed them from the slots, wiped them dry, loaded them into a different container, and then pushed them down to where other people packed them for shipping.

That was clearly a deadend job at IBM; I had no hope for advancement as an unskilled worker. I planned to work there for a while and save up some money so Deng, Akot, and me could move to a different state with a better climate. I worked there for nearly a month.

In December, Deng came back from his trip to Missouri. I told him, "Since you have now returned from your trip, let's figure out which state to move to, because I didn't plan to come and live in Minnesota."

We decided we had three options—Nashville, Atlanta, or Seattle. Deng leaned toward Atlanta, Akot did not care, and I favored Seattle. I wanted to go to Seattle because Lual Jala, my friend who had been in the refugee camp and Kibera Slum with me, had lived in Seattle since he came from Africa in 1995. He and I communicated over the phone ever since I got to Rochester from Job Corps. He told me that I should come to Seattle and not go to any other state.

I had asked Jala about the climate and job opportunities. He assured me the winter in Seattle was moderate. The temperature never goes below zero. With regard to jobs, he told me there were plenty of them. After I confirmed that information about Seattle, and Deng came back from his trip to Atlanta and suggested we should move there, I told him I was not interested in moving to Atlanta.

When I was still in Job Corps, I had spent Christmas of 1998 at Abraham Makoi's apartment in Atlanta and that's when I learned about Georgia, especially Atlanta. He worked as a security guard. He woke up very early because many jobs were farther away from the city, which seemed really spread out. He took a bus, a subway, and then another bus to get to work. He woke up at four a.m., but his work started at six a.m. with two hours' commute time every day. I witnessed that in

Atlanta, and when Deng suggested we should move there, I objected right away.

Atlanta was too big, and the traffic appeared to be a big problem there, especially during rush hour. I suggested we should give Jala a call in Seattle so he could tell us more about that city before we made a rash decision to move to Georgia. I called Jala and put him on the speaker so all of us could hear what he said. I asked him about all the things I had asked him before, the weather and job opportunities, and he elaborated on them while the three of us listened. Eventually, Jala was able to convince us to move to Seattle instead of Atlanta.

In the winter of 1999, IBM announced a big layoff nationwide. It did not matter to me, because I was leaving anyway. Many people were laid off at IBM's Rochester plant.

Chapter 27

Traveling to Seattle. A Hazardous Highway in Montana

In late December, we set off for Seattle. I had my Eagle Summit that I had left Deng when I had enrolled in Job Corps. Deng also had a black Ford Ranger pickup. We rented a small U-Haul trailer and loaded it with our bedding and glass coffee table. We gave away beds, mattresses, and couches. Deng drove the pickup, hauling the trailer, and Akot and I took turns driving the small car. We left Rochester at four p.m., took I-90 west, and drove for nearly four hours, 237 miles, to Sioux Falls, South Dakota.

In Sioux Falls, we spent the night at the apartment of Deng's aunt, Aker Benjamin. We stayed there all day as well. Then at around four p.m., we took off for Seattle. We drove all night. It was bitterly cold. In the winter, the trees stood leafless and looked devoid of life like ones on the Savannah in Sudan during the dry season. Everywhere I looked was covered in snow.

We kept on I-90 west. We drove through the night, across South Dakota, up to Rapid City, and through the corner of Wyoming to Montana. We did not sleep. At around eleven a.m. we were so tired Akot could not drive anymore. Deng swerved off the road because of sleepiness and fatigue. At that point, we had covered 862 miles in thirteen hours. We decided to stop in Bozeman, Montana, at noon. Deng suggested we spend the night at a motel there to get some sleep. He did not want us to drive to Butte at night. There was a high mountain pass that the Interstate went over before we got to Butte.

"Let's spend the night here, then drive over that mountain in the daytime," Deng said.

We rented a motel room and slept from noon to six p.m. Deng woke up and turned on the TV to check the weather forecast, which reported it was going to snow during the upcoming night. He became worried the snow falling might make the mountain stretch of highway very dangerous, maybe impassible. If that happened, we might be stranded at the motel for days. We did not have enough money to stay there for long. He woke us up, and said, "Guys, we don't want this snow to come before we cross that mountain, so we have to leave right now."

We agreed and left right away. Driving up that mountain was very scary. At the bottom, there wasn't any snow, but when we got almost to the summit, it was snowing. We were so high up we were able to see Butte, the next city, and all the city lights glittering way down there as if we were on a plane, which was about to land. I was so scared my heart beat rapidly, as though I ran a sprint. We drove slowly and cautiously, at ten miles per hour, through increasingly heavy snowfall.

Visibility was just several meters ahead of us. It was a tortoise pace. Deng, who had been a truck driver before and was familiar with that area, kept the pickup on the track of a truck that was ahead of us. Akot was also tailgating us in my little Eagle Summit. Snow poured down through our pickup headlight beams. Everywhere I looked on my right and left was a deep, dark valley. Dark tall trees loomed on both sides of the highway.

Even a small mistake, like swerving off the road, could cause us to roll off the hill and topple down into the valley. Deng drove very carefully up to the summit and then back down the other side. The city lights kept getting bigger and bigger as we drove downhill, which was very steep. As we approached the bottom of the mountain, it was not snowing anymore. The buildings in Butte kept getting larger and larger. I breathed a sigh of relief at that point. We passed through Butte and then Missoula.

We drove up a small hill. It was not snowing, but the road was icy and slippery. The trailer behind the pickup turned back and forth and, on top of the hill, the trailer overturned. All of a sudden, Deng lost control of the truck and it flipped. Both the pickup truck and trailer rolled downhill onto a hillside full of snow. The U-Haul trailer came off the truck hitch halfway down before we reached the bottom of the hill and went on its own way. The truck flipped three full times.

I was not wearing my seatbelt, so every time the truck overturned, I fell heavily onto Deng and kept falling on him until we careened to the bottom of the hillside. The clutch hit my leg hard and it swelled, but I did not feel anything. The front of the truck went deep into the snow bank. The truck engine ran until it stopped.

In the buried truck, abruptly stopped, it was so dark inside the cab we could not see each other. Right away, we began sweating profusely. We were dazed, and didn't speak for a few moments. I thought I was dead. Groping around in the absolute darkness, I pressed my nose to see if I was breathing. I felt my ribs. I thought I might have a wound somewhere, but I didn't find any injury. I finally asked Deng, "Are you okay?"

"Yes, I'm fine. How about you?" he replied.

"I think I'm fine too," I answered.

"Where are the windows located? I can't find the one on my side."

I told him, "I can't locate mine either. It's so dark in here."

We struggled to find a way out, but soon gave up trying. We saw the snow coming off the windshield.

I said to myself, *Oh, my God, I hope these aren't wild animals.*

The windshield cleared, and I heard people talking, as though from a distance. It was as if I had fallen down a deep, dark well and now people pulled me out of it. State troopers got the snow off the windshield and the windows, then they broke the windows and pulled us out.

Fortunately, on the opposite side of the Interstate, a passing truck driver had seen our pickup and trailer overturn. He pulled his truck over to the roadside and then walked through snow to the scene of the accident. The truck driver called the highway patrol, and within minutes, they helped us escape from the truck.

After the officers pulled us out, we were disoriented and could not immediately speak. One of the officers pointed out the truck driver, and said, "You're lucky. This man saved you. He was the one who saw you the moment you rolled down the hill and called us." On hearing that, we ran to the truck driver and gave him a big hug. If he had not responded the way he had, who knows what might have happened to us trapped in a wrecked truck buried in the snow.

Akot, who drove the Eagle Summit, showed up at the scene of the accident ten minutes later. He was so far behind us because the small car could not make it uphill as fast as the truck. Akot was surprised that we had had an accident. He asked an officer, "What happened? What? They had an accident, what?"

The troopers called a tow truck to come and tow the pickup truck to Missoula, which is home to the University of Montana. We got into the small car that Akot drove and he brought us back to Missoula. We rented a motel room and stayed there overnight. In the morning, we rented a public storage unit and stored all the stuff that was in the trailer.

A mechanic who looked at the pickup truck told us he could not fix it, that the truck was totaled. He told us the engine was "over-shocked" so it was not fixable. None of us knew what "over-shocked" meant, and he did not explain further. We thought he was lying to us. I myself did not believe him. I thought he made it up.

We did not feel comfortable. We stood out, and people stared at us. Whenever they looked at us, I felt nervous; obviously, there were not too many black people living there. A later check of US Census data confirmed my observations then. While about thirteen percent of Americans are black or African American, only 0.6 of Montana's population is black African American.

We worried someone might come to our motel room and kill us. We had heard vague and scary stories about those guys in the white hoods—the Ku Klux Klan. I am not sure there were any in that town, but we felt paranoid, nevertheless.

The next afternoon, we resumed our trip for Seattle in the Eagle Summit, leaving all our belongings in storage, except bedding and a few clothes. The stress from the wreck and our bad experience in Missoula combined to make us all on edge. Driving past the spot of our wreck, we perceived everything in our surroundings as a threat to us—the valleys, the snow, and the hills especially. Whenever we drove up or down a steep hill, I became very worried that something could happen to the car.

We finally made it to the state of Washington, stopping for some food at six p.m. at a McDonald's near the border of Idaho and Washington. Before reaching Spokane, we ran low on gas so we stopped again at a Shell gas station right off I-90 to fuel. However, when the young man working as a cashier at the Shell saw us drive up, he immedialey closed the store and told us we couldn't get gas. It was late, almost midnight, so maybe he was scared we were going to rob him.

I begged him, "Could you please let us fill up and then close the store? We are almost out of gas."

He said, "Sorry, guys, I'm closed."

We left and were fortunate to find another gas station not too far away that was still open. We filled up the gas tank and bought some drinks and snacks. From there we did not stop again until we reached Seattle. We passed through Spokane, drove through wide, empty landscapes and finally passed over the high Snoqualmie Pass, which leads down to coastal, western Washington. After the pass, the snow on the hillsides went away and we realized we must be close to Seattle; Lual Jala had told us it did not snow much in Seattle. We drove for a while after we passed over the I-90 bridge and through a tunnel, and before long we took Rainier Avenue exit around two a.m.

Numbers on the buildings confused us so we stopped at a gas station on Othello and Rainier Avenue and asked the cashier for help. Even at that late hour we saw children moving up and down the streets, and I said to myself, *Oh, my God, I hope these children are not selling drugs.* I had heard from Lual Jala that Rainier Valley is not a good neighborhood. He had told me, "Seattle is a good place, except if you live where there are gang activities. The good news is that if you don't associate with bad guys, you're going to be fine."

The cashier told us that we had passed our address a couple of blocks behind. "Since your address is odd (6727), it would be on the east side," the cashier said.

We drove back two blocks and found the building. Brighton Apartment is a big building with a fence, a parking lot in front of the building toward Rainier Avenue, and five entrances. We parked our car in the front parking lot and then went to the main door. Fortunately, someone came out the moment we arrived there, so we got in and took the elevator to the third floor. Coming out of it, we went directly to apartment #319 and knocked on the door.

Lual, who had not expected to see us so soon, answered the door and was surprised. "Oh, my God! They are already here. I can't believe it." We hugged him and greeted his friends who hung out with him in the living room. We sat there and talked to them about our long trip and the scary accident that had nearly ended our journey. At last, we were in Seattle and that felt really good.

Chapter 28

Seattle. Looking for Work

Word of our arrival and accident went around in the local Sudanese community like a bushfire. Jala's friends went home that night, called up their friends, and told them about our arrival and the accident. Then their friends went and told their friends as well. In Seattle back then, there was something in the Sudanese community called "breaking news." There were guys who went around, hung out with people, picked up any piece of information, and then spread it. The news of our accident took on a life of its own. In the morning, people came one by one, but sometimes in twos and threes, to inquire about how it had happened. We wondered how they knew about it, but Jalal explained to us about "breaking news."

Jala and his roommate lived in a one-bedroom apartment. Jala slept in the living room. Now that the three of us had joined them, we had to sleep on the living room floor as well. We spent a few days recovering from the long trip and then went and applied for food stamps and started looking for jobs. We were not hired right away, so we relied on temporary jobs for a while because we desperately needed some cash for nonfood items.

The first temporary employment agency we phoned was Onsite in Kent, Washington. They told us to apply in person. We did not know the area so finding our way was a major challenge for us. Fortunately, a

Dinka man named Isaac Dongrin—who lived in the same building and was also looking for a job but did not own a car—really helped us a lot. He knew the Seattle area pretty well because he had lived there for five years. We picked him up in the mornings in my little Eagle Summit, and then he showed us places where we could apply for employment. He knew the city and we had a car so it was good arrangement for all of us.

Fortunately, the Onsite temp agency found us a temporary job at Bank and Office Interiors, B&OI, located in Georgetown on 6th Avenue South in Seattle. B&OI is a distributor of cubicle stuff used in office interiors. Our main job was to unload and load items onto trucks for delivery and to move things around in the warehouse. When not doing that, we swept and stayed busy. That job made us look so dirty and dusty, as if we worked at a construction job.

Our supervisor's name was Paul. He was white, about five foot eight, and bald. There was only one black man, from West Africa, who worked there. At B&OI, we were allowed to listen to our radios in the warehouse. While I listened to mine, this African man told me to turn it off.

I asked him, "How come I have to turn off mine while you and everybody else are listening to their radios?"

"Well, yours is too loud," he said.

"If mine is too loud, I can just turn the volume down a little bit instead," I suggested, then turned down the volume.

At that point, I do not know whether someone had complained to Paul, the supervisor, but he came running and yelling, "Turn that thing off. Shut it off right now."

"Why are you yelling at me, Paul, while everyone is listening to his or her radio all around here?" I asked, though I complied with his order and turned off the radio.

Isaac, the fellow we were giving rides to look for work, intervened. He said to Paul, "Huh, what are you doing with Ater?" He wanted to fight with Paul.

I said, "Isaac, hold on."

Paul went to the manager, and Isaac said, "Let's follow him." We went to the manager, and Isaac said along the way, "Let's just leave. Let's quit."

Isaac was older than us, thirty-six or thirty-seven back then. In our culture, we listen to elders. When he saw that this guy was mistreating us, he realized this temp job was not worth being treated badly over.

I agreed with him. All four of us went to the manager and told him that we were no longer going to work for the company because of the way the supervisor had treated us was unacceptable and we couldn't put up with it. We walked out.

A few days later, I applied at the Seattle Goodwill as a donation attendant. Goodwill is a nonprofit organization that has been providing free job training and education for those in need since 1923. Luckily, they hired me in February 2000 and assigned me to Newport Hill Park & Ride station right off I-405 north close to Bellevue, Washington. Another donation station I worked at was by the Fred Meyer grocery store parking lot in Totem Lake in Kirkland.

Goodwill put cargo containers at all their donation stations. I sat in my cubicle and waited to receive donations from the customers and then loaded them into the container. If no one came, I read a book. Whenever the container was full, I called the main Goodwill station in Seattle for a pickup.

People donated all kinds of stuff. Most of them dropped off usable items that were in good shape. Sometimes they even donated brand new clothes. Others were difficult to deal with. Jerks cleaned out their attics or basements and brought junk to Goodwill instead of paying to take it to the dump. When I refused their junk, they became irate and often very rude. The smells were unpleasant—old clothes, old shoes. Forgotten items that had been in garages for years ended up at our donation stations, and then we had to sort them out.

One day, a man brought an old mattress to the donation station and said he wanted to donate it to the Goodwill. It was badly worn out on one side. It looked as though insects had been chewing on it.

I told him, "Sorry, sir, we don't take mattresses, but the Salvation Army does."

"Why the hell don't you take them?" he demanded. "Just take it, man."

He tried to unload the mattress from his old truck, but I told him once again, "We don't take them. Please don't drop it."

He snapped, "Who the fuck takes them?"

"I just told you, the Salvation Army."

At that point, he pushed the mattress back into the truck, and snarled at me, "You're lucky to have come to America so you can eat enough food. Go back to your country where people are starving."

I told him politely, "I'm sorry you feel that way, sir. Goodwill is not my business but an American business. I'm just doing my job."

He glared at me and then drove away. The next day, he came back again thinking he'd find a different person at the station who would accept his nasty mattress. As soon as he saw me sitting in my cubicle, he turned around, drove away, and did not return.

I had two supervisors, Parmajeet and Mahinder. They were both Indian. They and the lost and prevention people parked their cars in the Park & Ride parking lot, where a bunch of cars were usually parked, and then used binoculars to watch donation attendants. If a donation attendant took anything from either a customer or container and put it into his car, they provided proof by taking photos from their place of surveillance.

I came to recognize my supervisors' cars but not those of lost and prevention people; they all were supposed to be undercover. One day, I spotted a supervisor's car among the parked cars and pretended that I did not see it. I got into my car and drove around in the parking lot as if I patrolled the area. As soon as he saw me walking toward my car, he drove away. Maybe he thought I'd see him. If I spotted and identified him, he was done. I'd know who he was and he couldn't spy anymore.

We kept records of our time. I wrote down the time I arrived at work in the morning and the time I left in the evening. I had been doing that ever since I was hired. However, in one instance, a supervisor deducted twelve hours from my paycheck without my knowledge. I looked at it and noticed something was not right. I went and asked about it, but I was told one of my supervisors reported that I had been leaving work early. Therefore, I went and talked to the manager about it. He was skinny and had a bad arm.

"I'm missing some hours that I worked for, so I would like to get paid for those hours," I explained to him.

He said, "No, we can't pay you for those hours because your supervisor told me that you recorded time and left early."

I disputed that claim. "I worked hard for those hours. There is no reason I can lie about hours. Whatever a supervisor told you is not true."

He insisted, "It's true. You left early, we can't pay."

"This is my time. I cannot forge hours, and therefore, you do not have the right to take my time that I worked for and not pay me," I told him. "What the supervisor told you is not true. If it's true, please let whoever reported this to you come forward and explain in detail what dates I left work early."

The manager was adamant; he was not going to pay me. He stuck to what the supervisor had told him. At that point, I became frustrated. I told him, "Look, if I tried to cheat the company, God will decide between me and whoever told you this. But if you believe what is not right, and you think I'm trying to forge the time to get the money and you take my money away in this manner, God will decide between you and me also."

A look of concern crossed his face. "Are you going to shoot me?"

I replied, "I'm not going to shoot you. God will shoot you."

He said I threatened him.

I told him, "I'm not threatening you. I'm just letting you know what will happen to you as a result of the way you have exploited me. I'm quitting right now, but my time won't go in vain." I quit instantly. While we argued, people in the management offices listened to us. None of them intervened.

A week later, when I came to get my last paycheck, I heard from former coworkers that three days after I had quit the manager who denied me my hours got into an argument with the president and was fired. Whether they fired him or not really did not matter to me at all. I was determined not to work for them any longer.

A few days after I had quit Goodwill, I looked through a newspaper and found out that RichMark, a sticker label company, needed to fill a job in the rewind department. RichMark was located on East Pine Street and 11th Avenue. The job description was similar to what I had learned in Job Corps. Right away, I went and applied in person. They called me back and said they wanted me to come in for an interview. I dressed up in a suit, really looked presentable, and then attended an interview with my manager, named Paul again. This Paul was nicer than the Paul at B&OI.

Paul hired me in May 2000. RichMark paid me $8.50 per hour and a fifty-cent pay increase every three months, health insurance, and dental.

In the rewind department, we rewound big printed rolls that came right off the presses into small rolls, according to a customer's request, and then pushed them down to the shipping department. That job was very easy and didn't require any particular education—such as what I had received at Job Corps—but we had to pay attention to details. After one week of training, I got the hang of it. I worked for RichMark labels from May 2000 to June 2001, while I enrolled at North Seattle Community College.

Chapter 29

News of My Siblings

I have known Marco Chol since 1987, when he was the head of the Dimma refugee camp. Chol is a very educated man; he volunteered to teach seventh-grade math at our school at the refugee camp. He was not just an acquaintance; he was in school with my dad. After the fall of the Ethiopian government in 1991, I lost contact with him. Fortunately, I met him once again in Nairobi in 1995 while I pursued my resettlement process. He is a generous man. When I was living in the Kibera Slum, several times he had my friend, Lual, and me over to his house to have dinner with him.

In the early 1990s, Chol founded an organization in Nairobi called Napata, which provided subsistence farmers in Southern Sudan with agricultural tools, such as hoes and axes. For some reason, he lost control of Napata despite the fact he was the one who initially established it. As a result, life became very difficult for him and his family. He had a big one to feed. Due to lack of employment in Nairobi, he moved his family to Kampala, Uganda. Ever since I left him in Nairobi in 1995 and came to the US, I had remained in touch with Chol. Occasionally, I called him to find out how he and his family were doing and how things were going in Southern Sudan. We were very close to each other.

Staying in touch with Chol turned out to be fortunate. In June 2001, Chol found out about the arrival of my siblings—brother, Peter, and sisters, Mary and Martha—at a refugee camp in Uganda, and immediately notified me by phone about their appearance there. Right away, because

Peter, Martha, and Mary in school uniforms, Kampala, Uganda 2001

the refugee camp was not a good place for them, I sent them some money so they could move to Kampala, the capital and largest city of Uganda. I wanted them to live there so they'd feel safe and could attend school. I rented a small two-bedroom house and bought them a cellphone.

I got them the phone so I could let them know whenever I sent money. I also wanted to be able to advise them on what to do regarding their resettlement process to the United States. I made it clear to them that the purpose of that phone was not for socializing, talking to their friends or whoever. It was a means for me to stay connected with them.

After I rented the house, my siblings had a place to stay. I sent them money for school fees and asked them to immediately enroll in a school in Kampala. Martha, who was twelve years old, started in primary four, Peter, fourteen, in primary five, and Mary, sixteen, in grade nine. Once they had started school, I told them resettlement to the United States would not be quick or easy.

"The process to get you to the US will probably take a very long time," I told them. "For that reason, it will be wise for you to stay in school. I will drop out of college to support you, because I believe that is an important thing to do. I have already made it to college and can take off two or three years and go back later and still obtain my degree. I want you to take advantage of this time by doing well at school in Kampala so that whenever you get to the States, you will be able to keep up with other children in high school. I will do my best to get you reunited with me. It's not going to be easy, but it will happen if we have hope, determination, and patience."

It was strange talking to them over the phone for the first time. Imagine speaking to somebody related to you, such as your sister or brother, who you had never met. It was weird, but after several weeks, I at least could tell their voices apart from each other.

I had photos taken of myself, including one in which I was dressed in a suit, and sent them through the P.O. box that I had established for my siblings. Mary received all the important documents, such as immigration paperwork, via that box. She sent me all their pictures as well. After that, when I talked with each of them over the phone, I looked at their photo and was able to connect their voice with their face. It was like being together but not together.

I called them every week, sometimes twice a week. Part of our conversation was about getting to know each other, but our phone talks were more than conversation. They were a mixture of updates, encouragement, and advice on important matters.

In the beginning, they did not comprehend the process of coming to the US. They thought they were going to be reunited with me within a few months. They pressured me to speed the process up, get them over faster. As weeks passed into months, they asked me, "What happened to our form? When are we going to come over?"

Patiently, I explained that the process took time, much longer than any of us wanted. "It isn't as easy as you think," I told them. "This thing is beyond my control. This process could take years. That is why it is called a process. If it were under my control, I would have gotten you to the US in a matter of two months. I could have sent you visas a long time ago, but that is not how it works."

Trying to explain the complicated immigration process to them was very frustrating for me. At first, they did not get it. Eventually, though, as time passed, they became much more educated about how the process works.

After my siblings first showed up in Uganda in 2001 and I started helping them, the first form I filed was the affidavit of relatives. At the time, I was enrolled at North Seattle Community College and lived on Rainier Avenue in the Seattle area. I went to the Lutheran Social Services, LSS, office located in the University District near the University of Washington in Seattle. There, I spoke with immigration social worker Jan Stephen, who provided me with good advice.

"If your siblings are refugees, you should file the affidavit of relation," Stephen explained. "You can list their names on it. You will keep the original form, and our office will keep one copy of it. Then we will send one copy to the immigration office. You should also make sure your brother and sisters get a copy of it as well. They will have to come through an agency as the sponsor, either through our organization, LSS, or another agency such as IRC, International Rescue Committee. They must have an agency as a sponsor. Since they have UNHCR status, they can apply to come to the US on their own."

I had done my own research on the immigration website, and I found out that a brother could sponsor his siblings by filing an immigration I130 form, so I asked him, "What if I sponsor them through the I130?"

Stephen objected, "You really don't need an I130 since your brother and sisters are refugees. If you file I130, you will be the one who is sponsoring them, as a brother, and that will not be easy because you will be the one to pay for their visas whenever they are approved. Once they get in the US, you will still be required to support them financially until they are able to find jobs.

"However, if you go through the refugee application, what you are actually saying is that you will be supporting them when they get here in terms of helping them be adjusted to the new culture. For instance, you will be doing stuff like taking them to doctor appointments or finding an apartment for them to live in. They would be interviewed by INS, knowing they have a brother in the US who would provide them with short-term support when they get to the States. I think that is the best option for you. It will probably take you a couple of years or less depending on the situation."

I sent the copy of the affidavit of relation to Mary, the oldest of my three siblings in Kampala. Then we waited for the INS' response. As we waited, my siblings became increasingly impatient. Every time I called them, at least one of them asked me, "What is going on with the form?" Every time they checked the postal box, and did not find a letter from the INS, they asked me again about it. They thought they would be able to come to America in just a few months, but under the best of circumstances it was a long process, and after the September 11th terrorist attacks, all immigration processes slowed significantly.

It became apparent to me that the affidavit of relation would take a long time, so I contacted the immigration office in Seattle in October 2001. I explained that I wanted to sponsor my siblings in Kampala, Uganda. I was told to file an I130 form for petitioning brothers and sisters. Then I was told it would take at least ten years. That certainly was not what I wanted to hear.

"This is not going to work for me. My siblings are refugees and cannot wait that long," I told the immigration official. "In addition, having them staying there for years would take a toll on me because I am the sole financial supporter for them. I quit college to focus on getting them to America. I need to get them over as soon as possible so I can resume my education. Currently, I work two jobs in order to support them, as well as myself, here in the US. I cannot do this for ten years. I was told an I130 is not for refugees. It is for those who live in their original home countries and don't have a sense of urgency to come to the US."

The immigration officer suggested I file the affidavit of relation. I replied that I had already done that. I asked if I could pursue both ways—the affidavit and I130 form. He replied, "Yes, you can do that, but it will not make any difference."

So I filed three I130 forms for Petition for Alien Relatives, and sent them to the immigration main office in Nebraska. It cost me $420 for all three forms. I was desperate to get my siblings over as soon as possible.

Two weeks later, I received receipts from the immigration office, informing me that they had received the forms. They indicated on the receipts that I'd be notified once they started working on the case; there was a huge backlog of cases pending due to increased scrutiny following the September 11th terrorist attacks. The immigration paperwork also specified that I could check the status of the cases on their website using the case numbers.

After that, my life became much more of a struggle. My expenses soared. I lived in a one-bedroom apartment with one Sudanese friend on Rainier Avenue in the Seattle area. Using a curtain, I partitioned the living room to make it into a bedroom in an attempt to save some money. I worked for RichMark Labels then, in the rewind department. I started out at $8.50 per hour.

My paycheck for two weeks' work was about $600. My roommate and I split the rent in half, even though I lived in the living room. I ended up paying $265 a month. However, it was still more helpful than living by myself and paying the full rent.

I juggled bills and barely got by. I'd take the portion of my paycheck that I had designated for my siblings in Africa, and wire it to them them via Western Union. The money I sent them covered their monthly expenses, including rent, food, school fees, and medical fees, in case somebody became sick and had to see a doctor.

My sister, Mary, developed an ulcer. Since I had advised her to economize with the money I sent them, just to get by, she bought inexpensive food, such as beans and rice. Whenever she ate beans, her ulcer caused her agonizing pain. Sometimes, due to that stomach pain, she was forced to miss school and stay home.

Even though my income was meager, I was able to send Mary a little extra money to buy some fruits and vegetables. As my income was not sufficient to afford to pay for quality food for my siblings, I suggested to Mary that she consider quitting school. Due to her courage, determination, and desire for education, she persevered and continued in school.

"Brother, don't worry about what you don't have. Just send us whatever you can afford," Mary said. "We will struggle like this, but one day when we join you in the US and all of us will get some kind of job. At that time, you will no longer shoulder this burden. The problem here is that there are no jobs. If there were, we wouldn't need any financial assistance from you."

It was very encouraging to hear those kind words from my younger sister.

Because of all the financial demands I faced, I was in a constant search for other ways to make extra money. One day, I encountered a young Somali immigrant named Mahad, who claimed to be an independent business owner in the Britt World Wide organization. BWW is affiliated with Amway. Mahad asked me if I wanted to make extra money and talked me into registering under him as an independent business owner, IBO. Every three months, we traveled to different states for business functions. I was told business conventions were very important for me to attend because my success as an IBO depended on how much information I gathered at these functions.

Mahad told me the top IBOs who had succeeded in the business, making $150,000 a year, came to the business events and described how they had built their businesses. I had to pay for the bus fare, the hotel to stay in over the duration of the function, and a ticket, which cost more than $100 at the door.

Being an independent business owner at BWW was exactly the get-rich-quick business model I had been led to believe. I had to devote my time and resources to building my business. I also had to set aside extra time to talk to people to get them registered under me.

Every evening after work, we went and talked to people in malls and espresso shops about the business. My "upline," the person who had sponsored me, told me that I only made money if I had exposed the business to many people and then they redirected their buying power to the Quixtar website. When I was able to do that, I was paid a percentage. Since I was only able to register two friends, I was getting a $6 monthly check. Most of my friends did not want to get involved. They told me that they'd join when I got rich. After I had been at it for a year, I realized I was wasting money that I should be sending to my siblings, so I became frustrated and quit.

Through that business, I did find one product that alleviated my sister's ulcer pain. It was a probiotic, which supposedly contained "good" bacteria. The probiotic came in a powdery form, which you sprinkled on food. It was said to foster the growth of good bacteria in the stomach. I bought some and shipped it to Mary in Kampala. She used it for a few weeks and told me it did help sooth her pain, although it did not do away with her ulcer.

Chapter 30

Supporting my Siblings

At RichMark Labels, I worked forty hours a week at $8.50 per hour. Occasionally, I'd get a few hours in overtime, but the pay was simply not enough for my bills and the money I sent to my siblings in Africa. I decided to look for another part-time job. I was hired by a security company based in Tacoma, Washington. I was provided with a uniform, but I had to buy my own boots. The security firm sent guards to sites close to where they lived. I was living on Rainier Avenue and Holly Street in Rainier Valley in the Seattle area. They sent me to an Asian grocery store, Hau Hau, at Jackson Street and 12th Avenue in China Town. I worked in the parking garage as a parking attendant. Sometimes, the storeowner required me to do some patrolling now and then in the store during the busiest hours to prevent shoplifting.

It was a grueling schedule. At my fulltime job, I worked from six a.m. to three p.m., Mondays through Thursdays, thirty-six hours. On Fridays, we worked only four hours, from six a.m. to ten a.m. and went home early unless we had overtime. At the Hau Hau grocery store, I worked four hours, from 4:30 p.m. to 8:30 p.m., Mondays through Fridays, twenty hours.

On Fridays, after working until 8:30 p.m at Hau Hau, I went straight to the China Harbor Restaurant on Lake Union, where I worked as a bouncer from nine p.m. to two a.m. Fridays and Saturdays, ten hours.

After they shut down the club at 1:30 in the morning, people did not want to leave right away. For that reason, we tried to get them out of the club as soon as possible. Once they were out, they wanted to hang around in front of the building and in the parking lot as well.

When people lingered, chatting in groups and not leaving immediately, I'd get furious, but didn't allow anger to show on my face; I might have lost my job. I wanted people to leave faster so I finally could go home and get some sleep.

My coworkers and I cleared club patrons out of the parking lot; it reminded me of how I used to drive goats and sheep away from eating the crops in Sudan. When goats get the taste of peanut leaves, they refuse to leave unless you become aggressive toward them.

Similarly, drunken people loved to hang out in front of the club or in the parking lot for a variety of reasons. Some hung out to sober up before driving home, out of fear of getting a DUI. Some stayed to socialize with new friends. Others were guys who did not get lucky enough to find girls inside the club. They moved from group to group, talking to any girl they encountered. Those were the most difficult people to get out of the parking lot. They usually were the last to leave.

Once we had cleared them out of the lot, I jumped into my old Eagle Summit and raced home; if I was fortunate I'd sleep from two a.m. to eight a.m., six hours. That often did not happen. When there was a fight after the club closed and some people got hurt, I did not get home until about 3:30 a.m. We had to call and wait for the police to show up. On Saturdays and Sundays, I worked almost twelve hours, including at the grocery store, from nine a.m. to 8:30 p.m.

Many weeks I was working ninety-six hours. On Monday, I started that difficult routine all over again. I never got a day off—I worked like a maniac. Old people who hung out in the lobby of the building where

I lived made fun of me. Whenever they saw me coming home from work they'd greet me with, "Hi, workaholic." That got on my nerves, and sometimes I entered the building through the back door to avoid the retirees who had nothing better to do than just sit in the main lobby, keeping track of what other people were doing.

At one point, an old lady approached me, and asked, "Son, are you trying to buy a house? Is that why you work too much like this?"

"Not at all," I replied. "I have siblings in Africa who solely depend on me financially. I would rather not work so much, but the situation I am in compels me to work a lot of hours so I can stay on top of my bills."

I grew sick and tired of those people intruding into my business. I thought of telling them to shut up and mind their own business, but did not because they were elders. I restrained myself and dealt with them gently.

Due to my tight schedule, I did not cook at home. It takes time to prepare good food. Between jobs, I ate a lot of bad junk. My main diet consisted of hamburgers, sandwiches, potato chips, candies, and sodas. Because of a poor diet and stress of my hectic schedule, my health began to suffer. I had trouble sleeping.

I suffered from terrible headaches and felt tired and irritable all the time, even at work. I was grumpy and snapped at people in a flash, including the manager at RichMark Labels. At one point, in my troubled thoughts, I even fantasized about bringing a knife and stabbing the manager with it. What led to that was an Asian coworker named Luc who did not get along with me. He had no patience with my attitude and behavior. Whenever the manager assigned us a task, we argued over very trivial things; those arguments nearly ended in fistfights. Consequently, the manager called us into his office to deal with our conflict. The manager gave me a written warning. Since I had been written up, I thought the manager was on Luc's side. In my mixed-up perspective, I felt the only way for me to retaliate was to do something to the manager.

My behavior clearly was almost out of control. Fortunately, the management understood I was in a tough place. Paul, the manager, called me to his office.

"Ater, we want to keep you. You are a good employee and a hard worker. Everybody at RichMark likes you," Paul said.

They had ample reason to fire me. I had reached the point where I had become visibly unstable—I was obviously depressed, never happy, and did not smile at people or even say thanks, whether at work or outside work.

Looking back, I was fortunate that RichMark Labels alllowed me to continue working there despite the stress I caused my coworkers. The wages were not great—though I did get medical and dental coverage—but I was fortunate at that point in my life to work for such a supportive employer. If they had fired me, my situation would have become significantly worse, not having adequate means to support myself or my siblings in Africa. Out of desperation, who knows what I might have done.

One morning, while I was driving to work, I ran through a red light. I did not realize I had done that until driving another three blocks. I was behind the wheel physically, but mentally I was not there at all.

That incident woke me up to the fact that I had some serious problems that needed to be addressed. Nagging pain, headaches, not being able to sleep, and, most importantly, lack of concentration eventually prompted me to see a doctor. In my confused state of mind, it was not my behavior at work that compelled me to seek medical attention. Rather, I blamed everything that happened between me and other people on them. I saw myself as a victim in every altercation. When I could not sleep, kept forgetting things, and ran through that red light, I finally said to myself, *Please see a doctor. You might have something wrong with you.*

The lengthy process of reuniting with my siblings was constantly on my mind, and extremely frustrating. I wondered, *How long is this process going to take? What if they are not admitted to the US and I have spent this much time on it? When am I going to go back to college and finish my education?* All those questions were always roaming through my mind.

I did not share my problems with my siblings. I considered myself as a parent; my siblings depended on me entirely, and I did not want them to lose hope or be worried about me as they attended school and worked toward their futures. Since my finances were so limited, I could not afford a cell phone. If I wanted to make a phone call to Africa, I bought a prepaid phone card and used a pay phone. One day I called my siblings from a pay phone on Rainier Avenue at around eleven p.m. Pacific Time, which is about nine a.m. in Kampala, Uganda.

While I made the phone call, a police van suddenly pulled up near me and stopped. Six police officers jumped out of the van and surrounded me. "Don't move! Stay right there!" they shouted at me.

It turned out they were part of a police gang unit and they thought I was a drug dealer. I was terrified; I thought they were going to shoot me. One of the officers approached me and demanded, "What are you doing here at this time of the night?"

"I am using a pay phone to call my brother and sisters in Africa. I don't have a home phone," I said, showing the phone card in my hand.

The officer who appeared to be their leader seemed to accept my explanation. He told me to go ahead with my call and said to his fellow officers, "Let's go." When they departed, I was relieved but so skaken by the experience that I went home without making the call.

Dealing with my financial demands was very stressful. I went to St. James Cathedral Church to see if there was a way they could help me with some bills, but was told they do not help financially on an individual basis. I was eating lentils and beans about four times a week. Due to lack of money, I could not afford more expensive food such as meat, fruits, and vegetables. I did not know about food banks and learned about those at the church. A woman at the church office told me, "If you are sending that much money to your siblings, then you shouldn't spend any money on canned or dry food. You can get those at the food bank."

Learning about the food bank made a big difference in my spending. Since I was getting free food at the food bank I was finally able to afford to buy meat, fruits, and vegetables to better vary my diet.

Food expenses for my siblings were the highest of all my expenditures. I estimated that $300 a month should be more than enough to feed my brother and two sisters, but that estimate was too low.

After the Comprehensive Peace Agreement between South and North Sudan was signed in Nairobi in 2005, residents of the south were able to travel freely. Many people, including folks from my hometown, Rumbek, traveled to Kampala for a variety of reasons. Some went there to buy stuff not available in their hometowns. Those who had relatives overseas, such as Australia or the United States, traveled to Kampala so their relatives could send them money; at that time, there was no way to wire money directly to Southern Sudan.

Travelers to Kampala who knew my siblings stayed with them, rather than spending money at a lodge in the city. Even if they had money, those visitors did not give any to my siblings. They had heard that my siblings had a brother in America. There is a misconception, especially in my hometown in Sudan, that if you live in the United States then you are rich. Once in America, I had discovered the hard reality of that myth.

It requires very hard work to get money in the US, just like in other nations. There is no such thing as getting rich quick for immigrants to America.

Another factor that led people to stay with my siblings is my culture's belief in collectivism. In my culture, a visitor takes precedence over family members, except for small children. You cannot eat before you make sure your guest has something to eat. You cannot even ask the visitor to contribute, even if you are certain that person has money; if you ask, that is considered a disgrace to your family. Hospitality is a big deal in the Dinka culture. You can sacrifice everything you have for the sake of a good reputation. That means you have to share, no matter how meager your income.

When I was a child, I remember one day when my mom gave me some peanuts, but then the neighbor kid who used to play with me showed up. Since I had only a few peanuts, I wanted to eat them alone. All of a sudden, my mom slapped me, and said, "Share those peanuts with your friend. Please do not ever do that in front of me."

The combination of collectivism and visitors' belief that I was rich led to a constant stream of visitors staying with my siblings. That was a big reason I sent my siblings $600 a month. During the Christmas holidays, and when school started, I increased the amount I sent to about $1,000 during those months because of Christmas shopping and school fees and uniforms. I did not want my siblings to keep wearing the same old clothing and shoes and stand out among other children as a result.

In addition, the Western Union charges to send money to my siblings were killing me. Western Union charged $15 for sending amounts from $0-$100, $22 from $100- $200, $43 from $200-$400, and so on. The more money I sent overseas, the more they charged me. It's like paying taxes; the more money you make, the higher you are taxed.

In 2004, I was happy to discover Halal Money Express, which is a worldwide money transfer company like Western Union. They had an office in Kampala. Halal charges $5 for every $100 wired. If I sent $700, it cost me only $35 in charges, leaving me with more money to live on. They even gave me a discount when I sent $1,000 or more. When I wired money through Halal, Mary received the money in US dollars. Western Union charged a lot and they gave it out in local currency. Receiving the money in dollars is much better than receiving it in local currency. Mary was able get a higher exchange rate from local businessmen who needed hard currency, especially US dollars.

Discovery of the local food bank and Halal Money helped me tremendously. I was able to send a lot of money to my brother and sisters in Africa and still have a little bit left over to spend on myself. Since I was getting dry food free at the food bank and not paying higher charges for wiring money, I was able to afford meat, eggs, milk, and fruit and vegetables.

After nine months working two jobs, nearly 100 hours a week, with no days off, the anxiety and stress caused me to become ill. I went to Minor & James Medical Center on Boren Avenue and Jefferson Street, next to the Swedish Medical Center. The doctor who saw me was James Navais, a slim and calm-looking man. He shook hands with me and smiled; I smiled back; he was the only person I had smiled at for months. Dr. Navais greeted me with sincere respect and showed me incredible kindness and humility. "What's going on?" the doctor asked.

"I have a nagging pain all over my body and constant headaches. In addition, I do not get to sleep. I feel bad all the time."

Dr. Navais did a blood test, checked my kidneys and cholesterol, tested me for HIV/AIDS, and so many other ailments I cannot recall. The following week, I received the blood test results in the mail. Everything was fine. I was not happy with the result of the medical checkup. I thought the lab people did not do a very thorough job finding out what was wrong with me.

A month later, I went back to the hospital again to see Dr. Navais.

"What is going on, Ater? We just did some tests last month and found out everything was fine."

"You know, doctor, I am really sick."

"Let's talk for a minute. What do you do for a living? Where do you work and how many hours per week?" he asked.

I told him that I worked forty hours a week plus overtime for RichMark Sticker and Labels Company. Then I described my other job. I went through my entire schedule for both jobs with him. He added up the hours to ninety-six per week. He stared at me for a moment, and then asked, "Why are you doing this to yourself? How long have you been working that many hours?"

For nine months, I told him.

"Ater, you are not sick," Dr. Navais concluded. "You are depressed because you are not getting enough rest. As a result, your body has reached the breaking point. How long do you think you can continue working two jobs?"

"You know, I have people I send money to in Africa, my sisters and brother," I said. "They do not have any other sources of income, and that is what compels me to work two jobs. It is not that I choose to, but I have to."

"If you keep working like this for another six months, you will die," the doctor warned me. "You need to let your siblings know what you are going through or find other sources of additional income. I personally recommend that you should quit one job."

I liked the way Dr. Navais dealt with me. He did not say, "You are not sick, so go home." He confronted me as if I were one of his relatives.

His candor saved my life. If he had not warned me that overwork was the cause of my illness, I likely would have continued working myself to death.

After getting that frank diagnosis from the doctor, I decided to let my brother and sisters know what was going on. I called and explained to Mary the whole story. Mary talked to Peter and Martha about it. The next day when I called them, Mary informed me of their decision. "This is the conclusion we have arrived at. All three of us agreed that you should quit one job," Mary told me.

"How are you going to survive then?" I asked. "One job won't be sufficient to cover my bills here in the US and your needs."

Mary was adamant that I needed to take care of myself.

"If you keep working like that and you crash while driving around, then we will lose you," Mary said, adding, "We see on TV here that there are so many cars on the road in America. If you work one job, even if you send us a little bit of money, we are all going to make it someday."

It was very encouraging to hear such kind words from my sister. My siblings showed me tremendous love. Their idea that I should give up one job really touched me. That was why I told them what had happened to me and gave them time to deliberate. Instead of just complaining and whining to them about my suffering because of them, I confided in them so we could address the problem as a family issue. It wasn't about me; it was about us. I quit the security job and kept my RichMark job because it had medical insurance.

Chapter 31

My Siblings' Resettlement Case Rejected

In 2004, four years after I had started working on the process of bringing my siblings to America, the INS went to interview them in Kampala. We were hopeful that would move the process along and bring my siblings closer to coming to America. Soon after, on my way to work, I stopped at a gas station and used a pay phone to call them.

The first thing I heard at the other end of the phone was Mary crying. "Mary, Mary, what happened?" I asked.

Mary needed some time to compose herself. I waited patiently.

"They have denied our case, Ater. They have denied us despite all this suffering and hardship, with no possibility of appeal."

She explained that they had received a letter of denial. On hearing that news, I silently broke down; tears streamed down my cheeks. My disappointment was profound. After four years of hard work and sacrifice to bring my siblings to the US, was this really the end? The receipts for wiring money to Africa through Western Union and Halal Money Express filled up a suitcase. I asked myself, *Is this it? Is this a dead end? What is going to become of my siblings and me? Where are they going to go? How am I going to be able to keep them in Uganda and continue with school?*

My hope and dream was for them to join me in the United States so we could live together as a family. This news about the INS decision was very frustrating, but I refused to give up. In my culture, if you are older, you have to have a strong will to always give your siblings hope. I did not reveal what I felt to Mary.

"Mary, it is not over yet," I reassured her. "None of you should lose hope. It is not done, because there are so many ways I can go through to get the immigration officials to reverse their decision. So do not think that when they sent you that letter of denial it is over. I am going to go to every office here in Seattle, and I am sure I will find some assistance. Eventually, you are going to come to the US."

I spoke with them one by one, offering encouragement and hope. Then I went into action, going around from agency to agency. First, I contacted International Rescue Committee, IRC, because they too can sponsor refugees. I went to their office and explained the situation with my siblings to a woman there, but she told me, "Why do you want to bring them over? If Immigration does not want to bring them over to the US, then they can stay there in Kampala. You do not have to work for them. Let them find jobs over there and support themselves."

That answer upset me.

"Where are they going to find jobs in Kampala? There are no jobs there, and they are my siblings. That is why I want to bring them over to live with me," I replied, and left, concluding that woman did not know what she was talking about.

After immigration denied my brother and sisters, I became even more determined than before. If one office did not provide me with useful information, I went to another. I was impatient with anyone who was negative. If someone was not optimistic about providing me ways to get my brother and sisters over, I quickly moved on to someone else.

After several fruitless efforts, I went back to Jan Stephen at the Lutheran Social Services, where I had filed the affidavit of relatives back in 2001. I explained to him that my family had been denied by Immigration with no appeal.

"What do you suggest?" I asked him.

"Ater, I really don't know what to tell you and I don't have a concrete answer for you," Stephen replied. "This is an immigration case. Our office does not have the power to get the INS to reverse their decision. The only option you have right now is to contact your senators since you are now a US citizen. Make sure you check with either Patty Murray or Maria Cantwell."

He gave me the office phone number for US Senator Patty Murray. I called her office and set up an appointment with a woman named Sarah. On the day scheduled, I went to Senator Murray's office with my suitcase full of receipts. Sarah asked me, "What can I do for you?"

I explained to her that my brother and sisters' refugee case for resettlement to the US had been denied by Immigration with no appeal.

"I am here to find out why they were rejected. I need some answers," I said. "Through Senator Murray's office, I think the INS can explain why they denied their case. I can't afford a lawyer right now."

"Okay, I will email the US Embassy in Kenya, and once I hear from them, I will let you know," she told me.

I waited for about two months. When I did not hear anything from Sarah, I called her, hoping to learn if she had heard from INS. To my disappointment, she said she had not heard anything. More calls to her produced the same result. I was fed up.

I went back to Stephen at the Lutheran Social Services again; at least he was always positive and gave good advice. "I really don't know what this lady at Senator Murray's office is going through with Immigration," I told Stephen. "I am worried that the immigration people are giving her the runaround. I have not heard anything more from her and time is passing. I do not think I should be wasting time on it. Do you have any idea which office I should go to next?"

Stephen replied, "You should check your congressmen too. You do not have to restrict yourself to senators' offices only. You can go to Jim McDermott." He gave me the office phone number and address for US Rep. Jim McDermott.

I went to Congressman McDermott's office in Seattle and met with Rita, a staffer there who handles immigration cases. Rita is a people person. She was very kind to me and listened attentively while I related my story. I always carried my suitcase of receipts. "Please, look at this bag full of the receipts for the money I have been sending to Africa for the last four years," I said. "Now my brother and sisters have been denied with no appeal. I am dying. I cannot sustain this anymore."

Rita was sympathetic. "I hear you. I can feel what you are going through. I can tell you are desperate," she said.

She went into her office and got me a phone number and address for the Northwest Immigrant Rights Project, NWIRP, a nonprofit organization comprised of a group of attorneys who provide legal services to low-income people. They assist immigrants with immigration cases such as asylum and citizenship. Rita told me to go and talk to those people to see if I could find a lawyer to work with me. She assured me they would not charge me very much.

"I will email the US Embassy in Kenya," Rita said. "I know for sure that the INS will respond to my email. They will explain why they denied the kids, but from that point on, I cannot move on with you. You have to have a lawyer to work with you and then I will feed both of you the information that I get from the INS. Then you and your attorney can take any action you think is appropriate."

I went to the NWIRP office and set up an appointment to talk to
a lawyer about my case. Unknown to me, the front desk receptionist
had mistakenly set me up for citizenship training—she supposed
I needed help getting citizenship. There was miscommunication.
I came back on Wednesday, but as it turned out the training was
on Thursday. I sat in the waiting room for a very long time, from
ten a.m. to almost one p.m. There was a lawyer there named Bina
Ellefson. Her parents were from India but she was born and grew up
in the United States. Along with Rita in Congressman McDermott's
office, Bina would prove to be one of the most important people in
my life.

Bina walked out of her office and went to lunch. She glanced over
and saw me sitting in the waiting room. When she returned from lunch,
she saw me still sitting in the waiting room. She stopped and asked me
kindly, "Sir, have you been helped."

"No, I haven't."

She went and asked the front desk why I had not been helped yet.
She told the receptionist, "This gentleman has been here for a very long
time. When I went for lunch, I saw him sitting there. Can you figure out
what he is here for?"

The receptionist checked on the computer and then said, "Oh! He
has been scheduled for citizenship training, but the training is not today.
It's on Thursday, tomorrow."

"I am a citizen already. I am not here for citizenship training," I said.

Bina, who followed my interchange with the receptionist, then asked
me, "What are you here for?"

"I have a problem."

She could tell by my expression that I was desperate. I had been
sitting there for hours without anything to eat; only some water from

the drinking fountain. My goal that day was to make sure I talked to a lawyer. Bina invited me to her office and, once we were settled there, asked me what was going on.

I explained the situation to her—that my brother and sisters had been denied by the INS, that I was working with Congressman Jim McDermott's office and that Rita, a staffer in the congressman's office, recommended that I go to NWIRP to see if I could get an attorney.

Bina was clearly hesitant. "I usually don't do cases of this nature. Maybe I will connect you with some other people who can help you in this case," she said.

"For you to believe what I am going through is true, I am going to call my sister, Mary, in Africa right now so she can explain to you in her own words," I said.

I pulled a prepaid phone card from my wallet and used Bina's office phone to call Mary in Africa. I asked Mary to talk with Bina.

Mary explained what had happened in the interview with the INS, but then she started weeping and sobbing over the phone. "We don't have hope anymore," Mary said. Bina's eyes filled with tears; she obviously empathized with our plight.

The moment I saw tears in Bina's eyes I started praying with all my heart. I said to myself, *Thank you, God, for bringing me to this kind lady who values human lives and cares about the suffering and hardship my brother, sisters, and me are going through. Let our problems be solved through this office and McDermott's office.*

After they were done talking, Bina handed the phone back to me. I said, "Mary, I will call you back because I am talking with Bina right now." Then we hung up.

Right away, Bina went online and emailed *The Seattle Times* reporter Lornet Turnbul.

"We are going to get your story in the newspaper so people will be aware of what you and your siblings are going through," Bina said. "Maybe it will help a little bit."

Lornet agreed to listen to my story and set up an interview with me. The following Saturday morning Bina and Lornet came to my apartment; Lornet interviewed me in the living room. He asked me about what was going on in Sudan and what had caused my siblings to flee the country. The following Saturday they put my story in the newspaper. Since the *The Seattle Times* is the largest circulation newspaper in the state, we hoped the publicity would help break our impasse with the INS.

Rita had emailed the US embassy in Kenya and received a response. She forwarded the INS response to Bina, and called me, saying I should get together with Bina to hear what the INS had said about the denial of my brother and sisters. Bina told me the main problem was that the INS did not believe that my siblings were actually related to me.

I was dumbfounded. "How could the INS think that? They are my brother and sisters for real! Look how much money I have spent on them," I said, then showed her my suitcase full of Western Union receipts. "If I am pretending to bring somebody's kids to America, I wouldn't have spent this much money on them! But because we are related, I was willing to go through all this hardship and suffering."

Rita emailed the INS again, asserting that I was definite in my belief they were my siblings.

A few weeks later, the INS replied to Rita via email, stating that my last option was DNA testing with my siblings to prove our kinship. On top of that, I'd have to pay for it. The INS said if I agreed to that idea, then they'd be happy to reopen the case.

Rita informed my lawyer, Bina, about the INS' recommendation, and Bina set up an appointment with me once again.

"Ater, this is what is going on. The INS is suggesting you go through DNA testing with your siblings to prove your relationship to them so they can reopen the case," Bina said when we met. As she explained, her eyes opened wider, her facial expression indicating that I better be sure of what I was claiming.

"Bingo, yeah," I replied.

"Are you going to do it?"

"Of course. These are my siblings. You will see what is going to happen. I am so glad the INS is requiring me to do this. I have been praying for DNA testing for a very long time. I am so thankful that my prayers have been answered."

On hearing that the INS was open to DNA testing, I was ecstatic. I was convinced this was my best path to changing immigration officials' stance on my siblings. I was filled with incredible excitement; so full of energy and vitality at that moment when I learned the only thing standing between my siblings coming to America was DNA testing.

Two weeks later, I went to the Swedish Medical Center in Seattle for a swab sample. I paid $900 for the four of us. They took samples from me, which were sent to a lab in North Carolina for DNA testing. They did the same procedure with my brother and sisters in Kampala, Uganda. Samples from my siblings were sent to the same facility in North Carolina.

Getting results of the testing took long months that we endured with barely contained patience. When I finally received a letter with the test results, I cracked open the envelope with excitement and positive expectation. We were indeed siblings—test results showed a 99 percent match. There was no doubt now. I called my brother and sisters, Bina, Rita, and Lornet, *The Seattle Times* reporter, to let them all know the DNA test results. Everyone greeted the news with great excitement, and we all knew then that my persistence and arduous battle with the INS was finally coming to an end.

All my life, I have never accepted failure and defeat. Failures are like temporary roadblocks. If we learn how to get around them, eventually, we will succeed. The true failure is when we give up seeking answers to our problems. In life, what truly counts is the determination in whatever you desire to accomplish. If what you are doing is the right thing, go ahead with it, and do not let yourself be discouraged by temporary failures. Be persistent and you will win in the end.

Chapter 32

Cab Driving

Excitement on learning the DNA results eventually turned again to waiting. It took a very long time to hear again from the INS; it consumed all of 2005.

Since I had quit my second job, my siblings were not eating well. A Somali friend of mine, Bishar Ali, recommended that I consider becoming a taxi cab driver. Ali, who had been driving a cab for several years in the Seattle area, said I could make enough money to pay my bills. I had met Ali while pursuing my Amway business. Ali, a married man with a son and daughter, had figured out that I had financial problems when I didn't have enough money to attend Amway conventions, which were held quarterly in different cities.

I was skeptical of Ali's suggestion. I thought there was no money in the taxi cab business.

"Man, are you kidding me?" I replied to Ali. "I should quit my job that has medical insurance and drive a cab?"

Ali was insistent. "Please, believe me, I have been doing this for three years. In the winter, you do not make much money because of a lack of tourism, but still you can afford to pay your bills and feed your family. When the summer season comes, you are probably going to take home at least $4,000 net a month. In the summer, many conventions are held in downtown, and it is the cruise ship season as well. Forget about that job and start driving a cab."

"How am I going to find my way around in this big city? I can't do it," I countered.

"Don't worry about that. You will be trained on how to find addresses. Once you start driving, I will be there to help you out," Ali said. "Also, customers will be helping you, because most of them know where they are going. It is when you are dispatched to pick them up that you are going to need directions from me. From now on, get yourself a cellphone. Whenever you are having any difficulty finding an address, just give me a call, and I will direct you."

In the end, Ali convinced me that driving a cab was a good idea for me, but the fear of not being able to pay my bills still lingered in my mind.

With Ali's guidance, I contacted the Yellow Cab Association and paid about $700 for one week of training. I went to the city and paid fees for a business license and defensive driving course. The whole process cost me nearly $1,000. After I was done with the city, I went back to Yellow Cab and leased a cab for $420 a week. I can vividly remember that cab, No. 427.

In December 2005, I started driving a cab. Later, when the summer finally arrived, the cab business picked up significantly. Sometimes, I ran as many as thirteen airport trips a day. I made a little bit over $4,000 per month.

RichMark employees were very supportive of me. They had read in *The Seattle Times* about the INS denial of my siblings. The day after that story appeared, I arrived at work looking very dejected. My co-workers had read the newspaper story and decided to assist my siblings and me with money. That day, RichMark employees contributed $800. Paul, the manager, surprised me with the envelope containing the money, and said, "This is our support for you and your family. We know you are going through a turbulent time, and there is no other way we can assist you."

I was overhelmed with appreciation for their kindness. They had backed me when my earlier behavior at another less-supportive employee likely would have led to me getting fired. Now they were giving me money to help me and my family. It helped clear the bills I had been putting aside for a very long time. I was sorry to leave such a supportive employer with such good co-workers, but I simply had to make more money to support my silblings and myself.

After I had driven the cab for two months, I called my siblings and told them to look for a nicer three-bedroom and two-bathroom house with a fence.

"Are you going to be able to afford it? We should stay in this smaller house," Mary said.

"Please, do what I am asking you to do. From now on, you are going to be eating twice a day. I am driving a cab, and it is the summertime here. The cab business is much better at this time. Get a nicer place and eat well," I replied.

In my opinion, driving a cab is one of the hardest, most stressful jobs in the world. It is so unpredictable; it messes with your mind. Sometimes I'd get a customer who was rude, unpleasant, or bizarre. One I remember was nasty for no reason whatsoever and cursed me with the F-word. I had a customer who tipped me $60, which was three times the fare.

Having good people skills is crucial to being a good cab driver, and at the same time staying safe and making money. I read each customer's body language and attitude and adjusted my interaction with them accordingly.

As soon as a customer got into my cab, I greeted them in a courteous manner. If they responded, I continued to converse. If they were quiet, then I shut up and waited to see if they would start a conversation. If not, that was okay with me. Some people just wanted a quiet ride to their destination. It is important to respect that.

What I liked least about cab driving—aside from rude and abusive passengers—was that I had to constantly multitask. On the dashboard in front of me was a small computer by which the dispatch sent messages about people for me to pick up. I was constantly glancing at it. When it beeped, I pressed the button to either accept or reject the trip. Besides looking at the computer, I was also keeping an eye on quickly changing traffic, traffic lights, pedestrians who could suddenly appear in crosswalks and customers who flagged me down for a ride. All those activities were carried out simultaneously. I woke up at three a.m., picked up my cab at four a.m. at Yellow Cab, and worked until three p.m., eleven hours a shift, seven days a week.

Driving a cab is not safe. Taxi cab drivers have one of the highest homicide rates of any occupation in America.

As a cab driver, you are vulnerable because you have no idea what kind of person you are picking up. They could be the nicest person in the world, or a robber or murderer. I had a lot of sympathy for the prostitutes I saw on the streets. Like cab drivers, they had no idea what kind of person their customers might turn out to be. Numerous prostitutes were murdered in the state of Washington during the 1980s and 1990s by the Green River serial killer, Gary Ridgway. Obviously, the prostitutes he murdered did not know he was going to kill them. They thought he was a legitimate prospect. You can't tell just by looking at someone, or even with a brief conversation like I had with most customers.

When I started driving a cab in the Seattle area, my friend, Ali, advised me not to go to certain parts of the U-district, Central District, Delridge area, and Aurora Avenue North.

"Since you are still a rookie, pick up your cab at four a.m. and go straight away to Westin Hotel, the Hyatt, or the Sheraton and sit in a line with the other cabs. When you get a trip from one of these hotels, it will be a nice one to the airport. The people you pick up at the hotels are professionals who come for business conventions. They also tip well," Ali said.

"Stay at the hotels until I get to town. Then you and I can go and work in the neighborhoods," said Ali, who did not lease his cab from Yellow Cab as I did; he was an independent cab driver and could start his work day late or take off a day whenever he wished. I stuck to the advice he gave me.

Ali told me of a Somali cab driver who was shot near 23rd Avenue South & South Graham Street in January 2004. The driver was dispatched at around two a.m. to pick up young men at a Rainier Valley McDonald's. After they were picked up, they directed the driver to where they wanted to go. When they arrived at 23rd and Graham, they shot and killed the cab driver and ran away.

According to a *The Seattle Times* article, the driver's friends said he was a hard-working Somali immigrant who had come to America eleven years before. The driver worked for Yellow Cab only on weekends. The rest of the time, he was an instructional aid for Seattle schools, helping Somali students adjust to the American education system.

According to media reports, one of the young men told police they robbed the Somali cab driver because they were bored.

The instructor who trained us in the defensive driving course warned us about the dangers of driving a cab, and referred to the homicide of the Somali cab driver.

"Be careful. There are bad guys out there who want to kill innocent people for no reason," the instructor told us. "Keep your cab's doors locked all the time, because if you leave them unlocked, somebody can get in, and legally you cannot force a customer out of the cab. You have to provide service to them. Once they are in, if they are a criminal, they can tell you to take them someplace where they can do harm to you."

There were more hazards than dangerous customers. Within the first two weeks of cab driving, I was involved in a traffic accident. I picked up a couple at a grocery store in the Capitol Hill area, then drove down to Pine Street and turned right onto 12th Avenue. As I was driving north on 12th Avenue, a woman drove east and up the hill on Republican Street. She was talking on a cellphone.

The moment I saw her approaching I knew she was going to run a stop sign. According to what I later heard from police, she was from out of state and calling a friend to get directions. I briefly considered speeding up to avoid being hit, but had I, she likely would have T-boned my cab. She was going faster than I was. I slowed down. All of a sudden, I heard a loud noise from the impact. She hit my car just above the left front wheel. The airbag sprang out in a flash, hit my chest, and spat a stinking powdery substance all over my head and face. My customers and I were stunned quiet for a few seconds. I asked my passengers if they were all right.

"Yeah, we are fine back here. It's you who we're worried about because the impact happened at the front," one of the passengers said.

Initially, I thought I was fine, but I was not. A few moments later, I felt excruciating pain in my lower back from whiplash. The police showed up quickly; the accident took place about three blocks from a police station. An officer spoke with the woman who had crashed into my cab first. She blamed it on me, saying I did not slow down to let her cross the street. The officer came and asked me about how the accident had happened.

"First of all, I had the right of way. There is a stop sign over there, but this lady was on the phone, and I thought she was going to stop, but she did not. That is why I slowed down, because if I had sped up, she would have T-boned me, and I would have died," I told the officer.

My customers supported my account of the accident, that the other driver had run the stop sign while talking on the phone. Their testimony to the police helped me big time. The other driver received two tickets, one for talking on the phone while driving, and the other for running the stop sign. I did not get a ticket.

Because of my lower back pain, I went to a chiropractor and was treated for three months. I also cut down on cab driving. The doctor provided me with a belt that I wore while I worked. I found an attorney and filed suit against the other driver's insurance company, which agreed to settle the case without going to trial. They settled for $15,000; after the medical bills and attorney's fees were deducted, I eventually received $5,000.

By December of 2005, I had moved from Rainier Avenue, where I was living in a living room, to the SeaTac area and rented a studio apartment for $450 a month. Since I was making more money driving a cab I was able to afford to live by myself.

The first studio I rented was very old and dingy. The whole building itself was old. When it rained, the rainwater sat on the rooftop for days. After I had lived there for a month, water leaked into my apartment. I talked to the landlady about it, so she moved me to a different one. The problem shifted from me to the person who lived directly below me. Whenever I took a shower, it leaked into my neighbor's kitchen.

One day, while I was taking a shower, my neighbor knocked on my door. I didn't hear him so continued showering. Five minutes later, he came back once again and knocked on my door. "How can I help you?" I asked.

"Man, you need to be very careful whenever you're taking a shower because it leaks all over my kitchen," he said.

I followed him to his apartment and saw his kitchen flooded with water from my apartment. I felt bad about the situation we both found ourselves in, and suggested he talk with the landlady. Instead, he moved out of the building.

Chapter 33

My Siblings Arrive in the US

In September 2006, my siblings were allowed to come to the United States. I was stunned; the news came as a great surprise to me.

I had called my siblings to talk with them about other issues when they told me their flight to the United States had been scheduled for September 26th. I had assumed the INS would notify me, but they did not. I told Mary there must be a mistake, but she confirmed that they were flying to the US on September 26th. I contacted Jan Stephen at Lutheran Social Services to ascertain whether he had been informed by

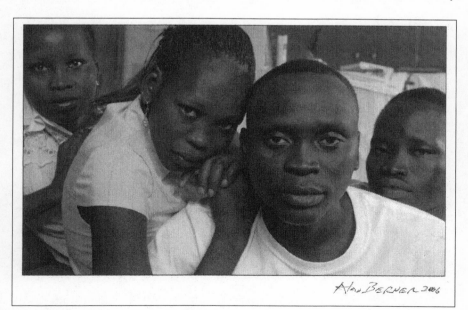

immigration about their arrival. He also had not been notified. Mary was correct—they were on their way to America!

On the day of their arrival, I went to Sea-Tac Airport accompanied by my lawyer, Bina, Lornet, *The Seattle Times* reporter, my Dinka friends, John and his brother, Sabet, and Maury Clark, a shaved-headed white man who walks with a cane and wears a hat. Clark, a retired investment banker, has helped many Seattle-area Sudanese in numerous ways, such as assisting with school enrollment, arranging doctor and counselor visits, and much more. Whenever a problem arises within our Sudenese community, he is the first person we call. We love "Papa Maury" very much.

My siblings were scheduled to arrive at nine p.m. at Sea-Tac Airport. Maury Clark brought a sign he had made that read, "Welcome Home" that we held.

My brother and sisters carryed IOM, International Association for Migration, bags. I spotted Peter looking very tall as they came out of the baggage claim area. I didn't notice Mary and Martha until they came closer.

All of us hugged one another at the same time. Maury, Bina, and a *The Seattle Times* photographer took photos of us while we were hugging. We wept tears of joy. I was so happy. My siblings were overjoyed and amazed that this was really happening. After so long, so many disappointments, they were now finally in the United States. Our dream had come true. After we finished hugging, they greeted those who had accompanied me to the airport. Clark got us into a limo, and we went to my studio apartment. My lonely studio came to life in the company of my brother, sisters, and friends.

As I saw us all together, I thought, *This is it. They have come to the United States.*

All the people who had helped me in this process and some of my Sudanese friends came over and soon my little studio was packed.

Lornet, *The Seattle Times* reporter, asked each of my siblings how they felt about finally being reunited with me and what they were going to do with their lives now that they were in America. They were so ecstatic about being with me. Peter told Lornet that he wanted to be a basketball player and that he hoped to study International Relations. Martha said she wanted to be a lawyer, because attorneys can make miracles, after the fantastic example set by my attorney, Bina, who had helped get them to the United States. Mary was undecided about what she was going to do.

Since I had not received prior notice from immigration about my siblings' arrival, I had not arranged for a larger apartment for us. The good news was that I was on a month-to-month rental.

Peter and I slept on a mattress we put on the carpet. The girls slept on my bed. It was very exciting being together. We talked late into the night, getting to know each other. It was incredible and wonderful—we were together as brothers and sisters.

They had stories of hardship in Sudan. Mary recalled how as a tiny child she had walked five miles to the "school," which was held outdoors under a tree.

"We practiced our writing and math skills using our fingers to create images in the sand, while hoping the sand would not carry off our images like a cloud," Mary said. "I learned to memorize information quickly, because it would be erased anyway, as we tramped home at the end of the day. As a child, I did not know that anyone else lived differently."

Peter had a similar tale to tell. In Sudan, children made notebooks out of scraps of cardboard sewn together. "We had no good facilities, but they were teaching us well," Peter recounted. "We were hungry to learn."

I lived with them in that tiny studio apartment while I continued driving a cab. If I got a trip from downtown to Sea-Tac Airport, I dropped the customer off at the airport and then stopped by to see if they needed something from the store. If they did, I took them to the store and then returned to downtown Seattle.

In the beginning, they experienced homesickness and culture shock. They missed friends in Kampala. They felt out of place for a while.

One day Mary asked me, "We just sit indoors all day. How are we going to get around here?"

It was a big challenge for me; I drove a cab seven days a week, and there was no time for me to show them around and help them acclimate to America. In the cab business, I could take a day or even a week off, as long as I had the money to pay the $420 lease fee by the end of the week. I wasn't in a position to do that. I needed the money then.

One day, after I got off work, I took them for dinner at a seafood restaurant on the Seattle waterfront. I ordered shrimp, and Mary threw up—she said it looked like I was eating insects. In Dinka culture, we eat chicken, goats and sheep, and cows. Animals with hooves are considered clean because they eat grass. My grandmother didn't eat chicken all her life.

All they did while I drove was sit in the studio apartment. It grew very tedious for them. Most days, after driving a cab for ten hours, I was already too exhausted to take them out. Sometimes, I brought them to the South Center Mall in the evenings and walked around.

Once, I overheard Mary say, "Kampala is even better."

I reassured her, "Come on, Mary. It's not going to be as boring as this forever. You will get used to it. It's because you're new. Once you know how to get around in the city, it will be very exciting."

The landlady learned that four people were living in my studio apartment without her knowledge and informed me that some had to leave. I asked her for some time.

"I'm sorry for what happened, but I have a big problem. My family just arrived from Africa, and I'm busy working seven days a week. Please, give me two weeks, and I will find a place," I said to her, and she agreed, adding that she hoped I found a bigger and nicer place for my family.

Within a week after their arrival, I found a two-bedroom and two-bath apartment at an apartment complex on 56th Avenue South in Tukwila, Washington. I drove my cab there, parked it right in front of the rental office, went in, and talked to Kim, the manager. I explained to her that my brother and two sisters had just come from Africa and all four of us were living in a small, dingy studio. I told her that the landlady wanted us out by the end of September. After hearing my story, Kim said, "I'm going to do whatever I can to get you and your siblings into a bigger apartment." I paid the deposit, and we moved in on October first.

Chrismas 2010, Peter, Mary, Martha, and me

Maury Clark, who had greeted my family with me at the airport, didn't give up helping my siblings. After we had moved into our new apartment, he invited us to his church in Snoqualmie, Washington; everyone there welcomed us with incredible enthusiasm. They provided my brother and sisters with clothes. Maury Clark took Peter and Martha to Foster High School and they enrolled in the eleventh grade. Mary enrolled at Highline Community College. My siblings started school a week after their arrival in Seattle. Classes had started two weeks earlier.

In the beginning, the difference in the US and Ugandan educational systems posed a big challenge for my siblings. They complained that the teachers didn't teach; just gave them assignments but didn't really go into detail about the material. In Uganda, they said, the teachers did a very good job in making sure students understood the subject matter before they left the classroom. Also, teachers in Uganda were not allowed to sit. They stood throughout the class period, which was forty-five minutes long. Since teachers in the US were able to sit comfortably in front of their classes, Peter theorized that some became lazy and pushed too much class work onto students to figure it out for themselves.

My siblings complained about moving between classrooms. In Ugandan schools, students don't move from one class to another; the teachers do.

"This is absurd and ridiculous. Why do students have to go from one class to another? This is very chaotic and noisy. The school looks like an open market or a town being evacuated," Peter said to me.

A big fellow, at six feet seven inches tall, Peter said other kids bumped into and jostled him in the hallways while hurrying to get to their classrooms on time. During the first two to three weeks, he was very stressed out about it.

My introduction to the American educational system had been different from that of my siblings. In Job Corps, where I took GED classes, moving from one class to another between periods wasn't a big deal to me. My problem had to do with the way exams are given in the US. They don't always directly reference textbooks and lectures, but often require analysis. When I was in primary school in Rumbek, Sudan, instruction was mostly about rote memorization. We were taught a lesson and then had to recall what had been covered. If you attended classes regularly and took good notes, you did well on the exams.

The US system is better than the one I went through in Sudan because it taught me to become an independent thinker. That form of instruction fosters critical thinking rather than pure memorization. Critical thinking is essential in problem-solving situations. During issues we encounter in life, we need the ability to use our brains, analyze, and come to thoughtful conclusions about often complex dilemmas.

After we had moved into our new apartment, a woman named Patricia called. Patricia, who owned a house in Edmonds, Washington, had helped Aguer, Jurkuc, and several other Sudanese Lost Boys by allowing them to live in her house while they were attending school. She had read about my family's story in the newspaper and was moved by the struggles we had endured.

"I'm proud, happy, and excited about the persistence you had to hang on to despite the INS denying your brother and sisters. I want to come over and meet you and the kids," she said.

I gave her our address. When Patricia arrived, she handed me an envelope with $1,000 in cash and a brand new laptop computer.

"This computer is for the kids to do their homework on and that $1,000 I have just given you is for you to spend on whatever you would like to spend it on. I'm very proud of you," Patricia said to me.

She turned to my siblings, and said, "Your brother loves you so much. Not just in words but by actions. All you need to do once you're here is to do well in school, because that is the only way you're going to pay him back. It's up to you to better yourselves in this country.

"This man put his life on the back burner for six years. He has been working hard for all these years to get you to the US while some young Sudanese guys like him gave up helping their family in Africa because of how hard it is to pay bills and send some money home. However, Ater managed to get you here despite all that. Don't take it lightly." My siblings were in awe of that incredibly positive and generous person. Her words touched me tremendously; I will remember them for the rest of my life.

Chapter 34

The Next Chapter in My Life. Returning to School

After my siblings were settled, I was at a loss—I was physically and mentally drained after six years of hard work with a single-minded purpose of supporting and bringing my siblings to the United States. Now that I had accomplished that, I took stock of my life. What was next?

I had planned to be done with college by 2004, but due to the lengthy process of getting my siblings to America, I was thirty years old and doubted myself; I was resigned to the idea that I was too old to return to college.

It took a lot of input and encouragement from key friends to change my mind.

"Don't give up after you have succeeded bringing your brother and sisters over," Patricia said to me. "It would be better for you to turn forty years old with a college degree than to become a forty-year-old man with no college degree. You should think about that for a while."

Another person who encouraged me to go back to college was one of my great friends named Moses Thon. He pressed hard on me, more than anybody else. Thon, one of the Lost Boys, came to Seattle in 2001, the same year I had dropped out of college to support my siblings in Kampala, Uganda. Thon was at Highline Community College back then and had watched me work hard and battle with immigration to get my brother and sisters to the US. When I told him that I wasn't going to go back to college, he was disappointed and disagreed. He told me that I should enroll immediately at Highline Community College.

"Don't worry about getting old," Thon told me. "You have your GED already. All you need to do is to find a part-time job. Four of you are living together now, so you won't be spending as much money. If four of you get part-time jobs, that will cover your rent, food, energy bill, and phone bill. Do not get cable TV because that is too expensive."

My siblings strongly encouraged me to go back to school; if I did not, they said that would be a big mistake. They asked, why had I worked so hard to get them to America so they could have better lives, and now it seemed as if I was giving up on my own future? They said all of us should pursue brighter futures, and that meant school.

When I heard my siblings' loving support for me, I changed my mind. I realized I was letting them down—as the oldest, I had to set a good example and be a role model. It took a lot of effort from friends, brother, and sisters to get me back on the right track. I'm so blessed to have loyal friends like Patricia and Moses, who care about me.

Throughout my life, I have prized education. It opens your eyes to possibilities. Of course having a college degree can help you make more money, but to me this is a secondary benefit. Lots of people without college make plenty of money. A college education develops your critical thinking skills; you can solve problems with greater ability and overall have more insight about life. If I fail to think analytically, then I will engage in simplistic thinking and make poor decisions, which eventually affect my family, community, and society as a whole.

After I had made up my mind to go back to college, I quit driving a cab, enrolled at Highline Community College, and applied for part-time work. I was fortunate to be hired by Olympic Security Inc., which is based in South Center in Tukwila, Washington.

I worked part-time patrolling the Puget Sound Energy, PSE, power station and grid in Renton; my job was to prevent thieves from breaking in and stealing copper. I sat in my little security shack, which had a radio, telephone, and a microwave. Compared to cab driving, the job was very easy. Every hour, I went out and made my round, patrolling the compound, which took about fifteen minutes. The supervisor usually came to check on me once a day, though not evey day. I had a watchman's clock, which looked like a regular clock, except it had a keyhole in it. Olympic Security placed keys in five stations around the compound. When I went out and did my round, I took that guard clock and went from station to station. The watchman's clock recorded the times I reached each checkpoint.

After I did my round, I worked on my homework until it was time to go again on my patrol round. It was a great part-time job while in school. I took three classes while working an average of thirty-two hours a week. Once my shift was over, I left the watchman's clock in the guard shack and punched out. Neli, my supervisor, read the tape to see if I had done my job. Neli, being a sharp person, noticed if I took too long between checkpoints or if I had missed one.

Before starting at Highline Community College, I was given the campus test to determine what level of classes I was ready to take. When I was a cab driver, while waiting for passengers, I used to read a lot. My reading skill level wasn't that bad, and I passed the reading section.

During the math part of the test, I really struggled and the stress got to me. I started sweating profusely, as if I played soccer in the middle of the day in the blazing summer sun in Kakuma refugee camp. It was not surprising that I didn't get a good grade in the math section. Since I did not test up to college-level math, I was enrolled in a pre-algebra class. The good news was that I passed the reading section. I enrolled in college level classes, except math, and registered for Writing and Geology 101.

Math was a huge challenge for me. During all the years I had been working, I had forgotten whatever I had learned about math. As a result, I was doing very poorly in my pre-algebra class. I realized I needed help and went to the tutorial center. Fortunately, I met Ed Morris there.

I raised my hand, indicating I needed help. Morris came over. I didn't know at the time but Morris had been teaching at Highline Community College for many years. I explained that I was having problems with algebraic signs and wasn't able to finish an assignment. Morris did his best to explain everything to me, but I still couldn't grasp what he said. I became frustrated and threw my homework onto the table. "Forget it. I'm done. I will never get this," I said.

"No, no. Calm down for a minute. I will make it easy for you to understand," he said. "What is the best way for you to learn?"

"I am a visual person," I said.

Morris wrote me out the algebraic rules, step by step, for my school work on a piece of paper. I appreciated the good advice.

"I can post these rules where I can look at them while in bed before I fall asleep," I said.

At home, I posted the rules on how algebraic signs change on my bedroom wall. Peter asked "What the hell are you doing?"

I explained, and Peter laughed and left the room. Eventually, I passed the pre-algebra class and went on to intermediate algebra. I continued taking classes at Highline Community College while living with my siblings. My goal was to stay with them until they graduated from high school. I didn't want to finish my associate's, AA, degree at Highline because I had lived in the Seattle area for a long time. After I had earned forty-five credits, I applied to Western Washington University, WWU, in Bellingham, Washington.

My siblings were all well-settled, so I felt free to move on with my life.

Moses had already transferred from Highline to WWU. I didn't know whether I could transfer to a four-year university from a community college before completing an AA degree until Moses informed me. He said, as long as I had forty-five credits or more, I could transfer before completing my AA degree. He also told me that he planned to talk with admissions officials at WWU about me. I was admitted to WWU in 2008, the same year Peter and Martha graduated from Foster High School.

In the summer of 2008, I took College Algebra at Highline with Dr. Helen Burn, who had received her master's degree at WWU in the 1990s. I went to her so she could help with a math problem. I mentioned to her that I was transferring to WWU in the fall.

"Wow! That's a great university. That is a good idea," said Burn, who asked whether I planned to live in a dorm at Western.

I told her that I might not be comfortable living in a dorm with students who likely all would be much younger than me. Since Moses, my only Sudanese friend at Western, had taken the quarter off to go to Africa, I did not have anyone else there to live with.

Burn said when she had attended Western, she had rented a room at the home of a woman named Sheila Mccorry. She found her former landlord's phone number online and gave it to me. "Give her a call and tell her that I recommended you to rent from her," she said.

After a few attempts, I connected with Sheila Mccorry on the phone. I explained that I was a student at Highline Community College in Seattle and was transferring to Western Washington University during the upcoming fall quarter, in 2008. I mentioned that Helen Burn, my instructor at Highline, recommended I check with her on any rooms for rent.

She told me she hadn't rented to lodgers for the past five years.

"I'm uncomfortable renting it out to people who I don't know very well, since I'm going to be living with them at the same house. However, if Helen recommended you, I have no worries renting out to you," Sheila said.

Sheila did caution me that her home was not real close to the university; in fact, it was about three miles away. Also, the house was furnished so I didn't need to bring furniture.

I thanked her very much. I told her I had a car, so transportation wasn't an issue, and that I wouldn't bring much with me.

The next morning, I rented a truck from a Sudanese friend and transported my mattress to Bellingham. When I got there, Sheila took me downstairs and showed me the bedroom and adjoining living room. I was so excited. The living room was furnished with beautiful couches, and was an additional place where I could study. The rent was $450, including everything—cable, heat, water, and garbage. That was an excellent situation for me—the peace of mind of being able to sleep and do my homework whenever I wanted was priceless. I paid a security deposit, and moved in three weeks before fall quarter started, just to be near the university and start to get to know the area. I also wanted to start looking for a part-time job before school started.

I could have applied for a work-study job on campus, but campus jobs cease during school breaks, such as the summer recess. Since I was not living on campus, I wanted a permanent job I could hold for a long time, without interruption, until I graduated. That way I could hold down my student loans. I had qualified for a Pell Grant and other financial aid as well.

Fortunately, after one week in Bellingham, I got a job. One morning, I went to a nearby Seven Eleven on Lakeway Drive to get a coffee and saw a "Help Wanted" sign posted on the door. I went in, got my coffee, and then told one of the cashiers that I'd like to talk to the manager. Luckily, the manager was there, baking chicken wings. She turned around and said, "Hi, I'm Julie. How can I help you?

"I am wondering if you're still hiring because I just saw the sign on your door," I said.

"So far, I have received six applications, but none of these applicants is an ideal candidate for the spot I have. I am looking for someone who would be able to work on weekends," Julie said.

"I think I will be able to cover that shift. I just transferred to Western Washington University. So this shift is perfect for me, because it will allow me to focus on my studies during the week," I said.

She gave me an application form, and I filled it out right away and turned it in. The next morning, she called me to say I had the job.

Chapter 35

Western Washington University

My life had taken a very positive turn. After six years of total focus on my siblings, they were fine, and I was able to turn my attention to my education. I had enrolled at a university with an excellent reputation, had a great place to live, and had landed a part-time job near campus.

Western Washington University has a beautiful campus with a lot of trees, up on a tall hill overlooking Bellingham Bay and out to the San

To my right is Chris and my best friend Nick McGuire, 2011

Juan Islands and the Canadian Rockies. The snow-capped Mount Baker rises over Bellingham. Canada is thirty miles away. The university is more than 100 years old. It is a busy place with 15,000 students, much larger than any other school I had ever attended.

2012

My financial situation was set. The income from my part-time job took care of my food, and the financial aid check that I received every quarter after tuition had been deducted went toward books and rent. To prevent myself from impulsive spending, I paid my rent quarterly. In

2012

addition to financial aid and a Pell Grant, I took out a $3,000 subsidized loan annually in case of emergencies. I put that money into a savings account. When a new quarter started, I used the money to purchase my textbooks in advance at Amazon.com at cheaper prices instead of depending on the financial aid check, which always came late, forcing me to purchase more expensive books at the college bookstore.

The first quarter was very stressful. I was new in town and had not made friends yet. Moses, my friend from South Sudan whom I had planned to join at Western, was away in South Sudan. In spite of those challenges, I adjusted well to college life and really enjoyed Western's diverse environment and atmosphere. At Western, students don't segregate themselves. Students intermingle with one another. You will see Asian students having white friends, and white students with blacks. It's just the right atmosphere.

With McGuire Family: Little Johny McGuire,
Shawn McGuire, Nick, and Paula—2012

After a few weeks at Western, I joined the African Caribbean Club, ACC, and made new friends there. In addition, I made white friends. My first white friend, and who became my best friend until this present day, is Nick McGuire. We had American History together—it was my first class at Western.

The first day we met was the day we both went to class and there was no class. It had been cancelled, but neither of us had checked our emails. From then on Nick and I became close friends. We sat in the front row of the class and studied together. The class was approximately ninety-seven percent white, with only three African-American students—one female and two males. The three students of color usually sat in the back of the classroom and, when the class was over, they left before I could talk to them.

However, Nick sat next to me in class, even though he is white, allowing me to feel at home. He was so nice and was interested in me as a person, asking how I came to America and made it to Western. His friendliness made a big difference to me; at least I had one good friend among these many white students. One day, Nick invited me to a birthday party at his place. At the party, I met his roommates—Kyle William, Andrew Taylor, and Max. He led me to great friends such as Michael Downey and Nick Nelson.

Initially, my major challenge was developing better study habits. Highline Community College is much easier than Western Washington University on several levels. As a community college, the academic demands are not as great as a university like Western. Many classes were pretty small at a community college and the professors were lenient on appointments. Since it is so much bigger Western has larger classes, particularly at the introductory class level, and the professors usually insist on office appointments to discuss a student's work.

Time management was another big challenge. At a four-year college or university, you're on your own. They expect you have learned basic study skills in lower grades and in high school, but I'd never had a very formal prior education. Sitting on the sand under a tree in a refugee camp was a lot different from the early educational experiences of most of my fellow students at Western. When I came there, everything was different and it was very demanding. I wasn't used to it.

Because of that challenge, I went to the university's Student Outreach Office, which assists students with how to cope and adjust to university life. I took a very useful class from one of the advisers named Joan Ulline, to learn about study skills and techniques. Joan told us to take good notes, to take classes seriously as soon as a quarter started, and to avoid procrastination on class assignments. She stressed that we had to read our syllabus and make sure we understood what our professors expected of us and vice versa. She talked about the importance of putting all the exams and test dates on a planner the first day of class. She added that we could look for big calendars that we could post where we could see them all the time. She told us to read the materials in advance; that way we would be on the same page with our professor and not lag behind. Joan's class tremendously assisted me in eventually getting my bachelor's degree at Western.

The first quarter was rough—I was very stressed out about classes. I asked myself, *Am I going to be able to finish my degrees and have any fun along the way?* That was just my academic life. My social life also was subdued— all the friends I had made were under twenty-one years old, and therefore, did not go to the nightclubs or bars. Moses, who I planned to join at Western, had taken the fall quarter off for his trip back to South Sudan.

Math continued to be a problem. On my first exam in pre-calculus I earned a thirty-four percent. I went to see the class professor, Andrew

Good, and asked what I should do. Professor Good, who is an excellent teacher, told me it was not going to get any easier since the second and final exams would be comprehensive. He recommended I drop the class. I did and ended up with two classes that quarter, American History and Biology 101. The following quarter, I took College Algebra with Professor Good. From that point on, I did not have any problem with Calculus.

The history class posed its own set of problems for me. Since all the students in the class, except for me, had been learning about American history most of their lives there was a basis of assumed knowledge I did not have. The professor was old-school; he did not provide Powerpoint or blackboard presentations. He simply lectured and asked questions. I went to the professor and asked for extra time on exams. The professor was sympathetic, saying he would be in a likewise difficult place if he had to take a class in the history of Sudan. Consequently, he gave me two and half hours during all exams instead of two hours. Because of the extra time, I ended up getting a C plus.

The next quarter, winter quarter, John Deng Duot, a Dinka, joined me at Western. At that time, Western became much more interesting. Sometimes I would hang out with him and sometimes with Nick McGuire. Deng and I used to go to Christian fellowship for a while. Then later on, I stopped going there when I got too busy with work and classes. Two quarters later, Moses returned from Sudan, and so I moved out of Sheila's house and rented with him and Peter Aguer near campus. Sheila's house had been a good place to live, but I enjoyed living with friends.

I adjusted to life at Western and enjoyed my time as a student there. Every quarter, before registration took place, I worked with my Student Outreach adviser, Joan Ulline, to plan the classes I would take. In addition, I spoke with other students about good professors. All of a sudden, the anxiety and stress I had at first just vanished.

One class that gave me a hard time was Management Information System, MIS. MIS consisted of two sections—the lecture and the lab. I didn't know Excel, and everything used to make a database was Excel and Access. I was still struggling with basic computer skills. I failed the lab and so failed the class. MIS was the only class I failed at Western. I retook it and passed.

Going back to Sudan was in my mind the whole time I was in college. Most Sudanese want to go home and help. When there was the referendum for South Sudan's independence in 2011, I went to Seattle so I could vote.

I had a somewhat eerie feeling when I was left with one quarter until graduation. I was finishing classes for my bachelor's degree in Business Administration from Western. It did not seem real until I attended the graduation ceremony and put on that goofy cap and gown.

My friend, Nick, graduated with me. The week before the commencement ceremony, Nick came by, picked me up in his small car, and we went to get our gowns, caps, and license plate frames. The license plate frame said, "Alumni, Western Washington University."

Graduation took place at 10:30 a.m. on a Saturday, but we got there around 9:30 a.m. to get ready. First, everybody gathered in Red Square—a main square at Western named after the red bricks of the space—before we walked in. As we prepared for the ceremony, I felt so emotional about the achievement of getting a college degree after all the hardships I had endured.

Looking back at how far I had come to finally achieve my lifelong goal of a college education, it was nearly incomprehensible to me. I was overwhelmed with emotions. Tears of joy trickled down my face as I reflected on my past life. I was and am so thankful to the American people, whose tax dollars in the form of financial aid enabled me to obtain an education. I also was appreciative of the American government

261

in general, especially former President Bill Clinton who saw the plight of South Sudanese refugees in Kenya and allowed some of us to resettle in the United States for the first time in 1994-95. Coming to the United States made my dream of getting a college education come true.

As I walked up the stage in the big auditorium to receive my diploma, I suddenly worried about losing that important moment in my life without capturing it in a photo, because none of my siblings, for a variety of reasons, were able to attend my graduation. Fortunately, unknown to me, Nick's mom, Paula, zoomed in on me from her seat in the crowd and took very good pictures of Nick, Kyle, and me.

After the graduation was over, I met Nick's father, grandmother, and grandfather, and Shawn, Nick's stepdad. I was excited to see Paula and little stepbrother, Johnny, for the second time. We went outside, and under blue skies, gathered on a grassy hill for more picture-taking.

In May 1985, as a nine-year-old child, I had fled my village in South Sudan as government soldiers attacked, trying to kill us all. I never saw my parents again, and wondered many times over the years whether I would survive to see another day. I thought back on images of war and danger, the desperation of flight from refugee camp to refugee camp, near starvation in the Kibera Slum, and, once in America, the grueling, back-breaking jobs I had suffered through and the struggle to be reunited with my siblings.

Now there I was, in 2012, thousands of miles away from Sudan, standing with friends on a sunny lawn at Western Washington University in Bellingham, Washington, holding my bachelor's degree diploma—another dream coming true.

My name "Ater" in Dinka has several meanings, but my favorite is "perseverance." I have tenaciously survived and achieved my goals in life, no matter the obstacles. I have perservered.

Epilogue

Although my childhood was devastated by civil war, coming to the United States gave me an opportunity to steer my life in the right direction. My goal was to become a doctor, something my dad wasn't able to achieve. I wanted to become a doctor so I could save peoples' lives. Having spent years in four different refugee camps, I had never thought I would have access to a good education and obtain a college degree. Fortunately, being admitted to the US for resettlement in September 1995 revived that hope and allowed me to look at life from a different perspective—one full of optimism rather than dread and pessimism, thanks to the US government. Coming to America, I still had to face many challenges, though, but those were not like the stark realities of Sudan, a daily struggle for survival.

I did survive and eventually achieved my goals through determination, persistence, and hard work.

My brother, Peter, earned his associate's degree from Highline Community College and received a full-ride scholarship through the College Success Foundation. In 2014, he graduated from Central Washington University, CWU, with a BA in Public Relations and a BS in Information Technology and Administrative Management. While at CWU, Peter worked with the College Success Foundation as a mentor for a former fostercare student attending the university. Peter also received a master's degree in Information Technology at Central on August 21, 2015.

Mary earned an associate's degree from Highline Community College and transferred to Central Washington University, where she graduated in 2013 with a degree in Business Administration with a specialization in Human Resources.

Martha has returned to South Sudan, where she runs a small market.

Relatives in Rumbek would like me to return. Having acquired an education here in the US—an education that is highly valued there—I'm expected to return home and help my community. Above all, our tradition requires the son of a deceased elder to take his position in the clan. Since my father passed away and he was one of the elders in our clan, I'm expected to take his place by uncles, cousins, and aunts.

I had such high hopes for our country with the creation of South Sudan as a new nation in 2011, but the sad, human tragedy there continues. The scourge of Africa, tribal conflict, erupted again into a new civil war, this time in South Sudan. It did not take long for civil war to rage between soldiers loyal to the South Sudan President, Salva Kiir, an ethnic Dinka, and former vice president, Riek Machar, an ethnic Nuer. The result has been still another civil war with civilians again the innocent victims. The new turmoil has killed thousands and driven more than a million people from their homes. Many are starving. I love my country, but I fear for its future.

South Sudan is very rich in resources. Apart from oil and other minerals, the land is arable, and people can sustain their lives as subsistence farmers by growing their own crops. Some day I might go home and create a business to help the country and its people.

Creating a successful business in the midst of civil war simply will not work. Since South Sudan is not stable, I will continue to live in the United States and wait for the right time, and pray for the people of South Sudan. We are a great people who deserve peace and prosperity.

Acknowledgements

There are many people I deeply appreciate for their help in pulling together this book.

I believe my friendships at Western Washington University happened for a reason. I never thought of writing my story until my friend, Michael Downey, suggested I should write a book about my life. When he told me that, I objected, saying, "Michael, I don't think I can write a book. Writing a book is not that easy. Furthermore, English is my second language."

We started outlining it and began writing, but he went on a trip to Egypt, and I was left with no one to help me. However, my friend, Nick McGuire, told me, "Ater, talk to my friend Nick Nelson and see if he can help you. He is an English major."

Despite being busy with papers and a portfolio, Nick Nelson agreed to help with my writing, but I still needed someone who had more advanced skills to organize my manuscript. Since I was a student, I did not have the wherewithal to hire an experienced professional writer. A couple of professional writers I consulted wanted to charge me approximately $25 per hour. I kept chanting every morning and evening before I went to bed to find someone to help me organize my story into a finished manuscript. I wrote that goal on a piece of paper and looked at it while chanting.

It did not take long before my prayer was answered. Mary Gallagher, editor of Western's *Window Magazine,* had learned about me from Dr. Kunle Okikutu, an assistant vice president at Western, and she hired

Peter Jenson, who used to hang out with my roommate, Dane Guetlin, to write my story for the university magazine. Peter Jensen had received his bachelor's degree in Journalism from Western and had worked for *The Bellingham Herald,* the daily newspaper in Bellingham. Peter reviewed my writing and interviewed me; he wrote an interesting story for *Window Magazine.*

Right after Western published the article, I contacted Paul Cocke, the director of the Office of Communications and Marketing at Western, to see about finding someone to organize my manuscript. Paul, a former newspaper editor, was so helpful to me. He said, "We will make sure you get the assistance you need, Ater. Just give me some time to talk to the English Department to see if they can find a student who would be willing to help you."

I was so excited that day when Paul told me that. I could tell from his face that he meant what he had said and that he was sincere and serious about it.

A couple of weeks later, I received an email from Paul, saying he had found a student named Marilyn Bruce who was interested in working with me, but not until after spring quarter because she was busy working on her master's thesis. I waited patiently until spring quarter was over and then sent an email to Marilyn to see if she was available to start working with me on my manuscript. She promptly replied to my email, and so we set up a meeting at The Woods Coffee shop in downtown Bellingham. When we met, I explained to her that I desperately needed her skill and talent to organize it into a manuscript.

Before we met at the coffee shop to talk about the project, I thought Marilyn might lean toward charging me to work on the manuscript, like other writers I had previously contacted. I offered to pay her for her time, but she declined, saying she liked to help people and simply wanted to volunteer her time. That told me a lot about her—Marilyn is a wonderful person. Now I have become a good friend to her and her fiancé, Ron Brandt, now a husband. I pray Marilyn has great success in her life. Good people with a heart like Marilyn's always make a difference in people's lives. She did in mine.

I'd also like to thank my friend, Paul Cocke, for everything he helped me with, including finding Marilyn to organized my manuscript.

I'd also like to thank *The Seattle Times*, for their generosity in providing a photo of the reunion of my siblings and me.

I'd like to thank Marisa Chenery, for editing my manuscript.

Most of all, I'd like to thank my siblings, Peter, Mary, and Martha, who have provided me with so much hope and love.

from left to right: Robert Omwanda, Ater Malath, and Evance Wekesa

Made in the USA
San Bernardino, CA
19 May 2018